CATCH
OF THE
DAY

Chris Schrader

This book is dedicated to...

Dr. Vic Pentz who has shown me that no fish is "too small."

Dr. John Piper who has shown me the foundational reason for fishing: "to spread a passion for the supremacy of God for the joy of all peoples."

Dr. Alan Meenan who has shown me to unapologetically stand firm on the eternal, unchanging truths of God's Word.

Dr. Terry Teykl who has shown me the power of fishing with prayer.

My wife, Lea, who has shown me the power of fishing with grace and compassion.

Our daughters, Maddee and Bree, who have recently joined the family fishing venture.

Our Lord and Savior, Jesus Christ, who called us unto Him and has allowed each of us to join in on the greatest fishing expedition of all time. To Him alone be the glory and honor forever and ever. Amen!

Table of Contents

Foreword

I knew Chris Schrader when he was still circling the bait. Hardly the most religious kid in the room, Chris was a bright, questioning teenager in the youth group I pastored amidst the beach-surfing-party scene of a sun-kissed California coastal community in the 1970s. When we met years later in Texas, it was apparent that Chris had been "hooked" by Christ and His gospel in a marvelous way.

Not long ago I was having lunch in a restaurant in East Jerusalem when I spotted on the wall an old back-and-white photo of a fisherman casting his net on the Sea of Galilee. After I finished eating, I went to the manager and bought it off the wall—at not inconsiderable cost, I might add. What enthralled me was not the picture's obvious religious significance, but the sight of the man throwing the net.

Frozen in time is the split second when his powerful body uncoils to full extension. His hands are flung high in the air. The net wafts in a wide arc across the lake. It reminds me of photos of Michael Jordan in midair. Passion, energy, and skill converge in a moment of raw grace and intense beauty.

In contrast to our Western understanding of fishing as sitting passively for hours merely "drowning worms," this photo, now prominently displayed in my office, shows what Jesus had in mind when he said, "I will make you fishers of men." He was saying, "Won't you bring your very best, your passion and unique strengths, to the enterprise of bringing people to me?" You will find this book is written in the spirit of my photograph. Chris Schrader makes me want to be an evangelist.

Not even the disciples were thrilled by the task of evangelism. Atop the mount of ascension Jesus told his disciples, "You shall be my witnesses...." But not until a couple of angels came down out of heaven and coaxed them off the mountaintop did they go down to Jerusalem. And then their feet stayed glued to Jerusalem until persecution forcibly scattered them to the ends of the earth.

Many of us can relate to the disciples' reluctance. If we were to rank life's experiences in descending order of the pleasure they bring us, evangelism might appear down somewhere near oral surgery and other things sane people avoid. Many of us have lapsed into what was known in the old days as "Clairol Christianity" (only God knows for sure). Intimidated and insecure, we keep our hooks out of the water. My Presbyterian denomination is famous for this. Once a Presbyterian leader serving on a panel was asked a question from the floor, "What would you say has been the greatest contribution by Presbyterians in the area of evangelism?" The man thought for a moment and said, "Restraint."

Consequently, we have delegated evangelism to a certain type of Christian—the sweaty revival preacher, the zealot on the street corner, or that wild and wooly character with the rainbow-colored wig who shows up at televised sporting events with John 3:16 emblazoned on his shirt.

The excesses of a few do not excuse the rest of us. If anything, they heighten our responsibility and compel our involvement in the great fishing expedition. There are basically two kinds of evangelism—confrontational and relational.

Confrontational evangelism is an all-or-nothing encounter that pushes a person to receive Christ right then and there and attempts to "close the deal," as it were, on the spot. In my younger years I had a lot of experience with this approach. I've done door-to-door calling, open air meetings, and campus blitzes with Four Spiritual Law booklets. I have two conclusions. First, thank God for confrontational evangelism. The apostle Peter was the master of this genre, salty as an anchovy. On the day of Pentecost in Acts 2, Peter proclaimed, "Would you like to know why the Messiah isn't here? Because you killed him!" It was perfect for that setting. His hearers were "cut to the heart" and three thousand came to Christ.

On the other hand, thank God for other options. In Luke 5, Matthew, the tax collector, wanted to reach his peers with the gospel. How did he do it? The way business people still influence their colleagues—over lunch. At the banquet for all his tax collecting friends, Matthew introduced them to Jesus Christ. His evangelism was one of networking, the American Express Card, friendship, and hospitality.

This book is more for Matthews than for Peters. Chris reflects a point of view that sees evangelism less confrontationally and more relationally. In relational evangelism the idea is that God has placed us as Christians within our network of relationships, family, work, and neighborhood for the supernatural purpose of living out our lives before unchurched people. Our genuine concern for these people with whom we share our lives will open doors for the gospel, if we will take advantage of them.

Opportunities for relational evangelism arise every day. In the car pool, on the racquetball court, in the parking lot after the noon service club breaks up, over the back fence with a neighbor, or over coffee with a friend. When the average church member talks to her unchurched friend about the joy of knowing Jesus—simply, naturally and enthusiastically—she fulfills the command, "You shall be my witnesses."

Once God has a willing witness, He will put that person in a place. "You shall be my witnesses in Jerusalem, and in all

Judea, and Samaria and to the end of the earth." The picture here is of a pebble tossed in a pond and the resulting, concentric circles expanding outward from it. Each of those ripples carried the gospel into a different cultural context. Jerusalem and Judea were populated with Jews, Samaria with half-breed Jews called Samaritans, and the rest of the earth with Gentiles of every breed and stripe. Even today, mission strategists still talk about "contextualization," how we need to adapt our methods to the context where we proclaim the gospel—be it Jerusalem, or Judea or Los Angeles or Amarillo. Yes, Christ is the answer for all people always and everywhere, but I have to connect my Christ answer to the heart questions of people within their context.

During seminary I spent my summers doing beach ministry on the sands of La Jolla, California. My context was the beach culture where I felt God leading me to reach out to the surfing population. After much prayer, reflection, and cultivation of my suntan, I founded a program called Soup for Surfers. With the help of some of the ladies in my church, I and my team headed to a hot surfing spot early each morning armed with a big pot of homemade soup. As the exhausted surfers dragged themselves on to the beach, teeth chattering and muscles quivering, we met them with a steaming cup of relief. Invariably, one would get around to asking, "Why are you guys doing this?" We told them that Jesus "grooved on" the spray of the ocean in his face (this was in the 70s), and that He would live inside of them if they would accept Him as Savior and Lord.

Years after that summer, I met a law student in Washington, D. C. who had surfed that La Jolla beach and remembered the soup ministry. He had since become a Christian. In order to be effective witnesses, we entered the context, discovered the felt needs, and while meeting them, we shared the gospel.

What are the needs in your context today? Most areas are plagued with drugs, alcohol and violence in all strata of society, loneliness epidemics in nursing homes and school campuses, and all manner of fears afflicting all kinds of people—economic fear, health fear, fear of aging, fear of dying. Many are emotionally paralyzed by stress, fatigue, or guilt. Henry David Thoreau put it best when he said, "Most men live lives of quiet depression."

So the needs are overwhelming, but when God sends a person into a place, He sends them with power. When Jesus commissioned His disciples, He instructed them first to wait, saying, "You shall receive power." In other words, "I will supercharge your ordinary words with My extraordinary power." It is said that evangelists are like turtles; they never get anywhere unless they stick their necks out. God will do His part if we will do ours.

Finally, with the person, place, and power, God gives us the prototype. "You shall be my witnesses." Christ is our model. Says John Stott in *The Mission of the Christian Church,* our motto is, "Even as the Father has sent me, even so I send you." To evangelize is to Emmanuelize, to disclose God with us in the midst of life.

Chris Schrader's great gift to the church lies in helping us do just that. He opens up new ways for us to become fishers of men and women, with integrity and intelligence, within our unique personalities and culture.

"Be sure your face is toward the light.
Study the fish's curious ways;
Then keep yourself well out of sight
And cherish patience all your days."

F. W. Boram in Isaak Walton's The Complete Angler

Dr. Victor Pentz
Sr. Pastor
First Presbyterian Church—Houston

Introduction

Ten years ago I went on a fishing trip that forever changed my perspective on evangelism. At 30 years of age, I was the senior member on the expedition. The average age of my partners was nineteen. They possessed one year of college—one year of attempts at independent thinking, one year of a myriad of messages about "life, liberty, and the pursuit of happiness."

About eight other fishing parties in addition to our little group descended on the target zone simultaneously. "Okay. You know what to do," the organizer bellowed as a final word of encouragement to the nine teams. "We've got our plan of attack. Now it's time to reach out for Jesus! Time to get out of your comfort zone, folks. This is for the Savior!"

The holy huddle was over and we proceeded on our mission. The only problem was I had never in my life seen so many unsure, unwilling participants on a fishing trip.

Don't get me wrong; these young men desired to draw people towards God's kingdom. Their hearts were right. They simply were not comfortable about the method with which we were supposed to fish.

We walked for five minutes without saying a word. I broke the silence with one simple question that eventually led me to write this book: "What do you guys think about how we have been told to witness?" The floodgates of conversation opened.

For the two hours that followed, instead of "cold contacting prospective clients" (as one young man summarized our mission), our little band of eight prayed, discussed methods the Master used, and alleviated misgivings about feeling like failures.

These fourteen meditations have been written for people like my former fishing buddies—people who feel overwhelmed by human methods that are all too often disseminated as doctrine by experts on evangelism.

What is the best way to be a "fisher for men"? The Four Spiritual Laws, Evangelism Explosion, Friendship Evangelism? That question is tantamount to asking whether the one who uses a standard rod and reel or the one who prefers fly-fishing is the best fisherman. Which is best to fish in, saltwater, mountain streams, or lakes?

Is there truly a best evangelism method to use? Or should we be looking at principles used by the Prince of Peace and His little band of fisherman?

The last decade's advances in technology have brought further questions—and misgivings—regarding equipment needed to fish. "What happens if I don't have a computer? Certainly you can't do anything without a modem, a mouse, a fax, e-mail, or a net server, can you? How did Jesus fish without a dayplanner? I'm no Billy Graham. I don't think I have the gift of evangelism. What's a direct-link satellite hookup anyway? Does anybody fish one-on-one anymore?"

It is my fervent prayer that all who read this book and watch how the Master and His disciples fished will be put at ease, inspired, and challenged.

Jesus and the disciples did not use just one method of fishing. We do not have to either. We have been given freedom in fishing! May these fourteen weekly meditations help set you free to use your unique blend of spiritual gifts, personalities, passions, and experiences to join the greatest fishing expedition of all time!

Chris Schrader

Scripture

Many have undertaken to draw up an account of the things that have been fulfilled among us, just as they were handed down to us by those who from the first were eyewitnesses and servants of the word. Therefore, since I myself have carefully investigated everything from the beginning, it seemed good also to me to write an orderly account for you, most excellent Theophilus, so that you may know the certainty of the things you have been taught. (Luke 1:1-4)

One

Fishing
with the
Facts

"I don't have a problem believing that God exists," said the thirty-something astrophysicist. "In fact," he went on to say, "most scientists I know believe the same way. It would take more faith on our parts to believe that the universe as we know it was formed completely by random chance."

This was not the response I was expecting when I received the challenge to respond to my faith. After all, I had grown up being taught that most scientists were undeniably opposed to the supernatural. They were supposed to have the "if-you-can't-prove-it-by-the-scientific method-then-I-don't-want-to-hear-it" mentality.

"The existence of a god, a designer, is not a problem. The problem is that people like yourself, Christians, claim that the only way to God is through Jesus Christ."

"True," I responded. "In the Gospel of John, Jesus states that very thing in chapter 14, verse 6: 'I am the way, the truth, and the life. No one can come to the Father except through me' (NLT). It is not really we Christians who make this claim, but rather Jesus Himself. We are simply relaying the facts as presented in the Bible."

"It still smacks of supreme arrogance," he countered. "What makes Christianity so special that it can relegate all other religions of the world useless, and their followers lost?"

"Jesus."

"That's your answer?!"

"Yes," I said with confidence. "Jesus is what makes Christianity so special. Consider these facts from a book by Josh McDowell called *A Ready Defense*, and tell me if any other religion can make such a claim about its savior."

> In the Old Testament there are sixty major messianic prophecies and approximately 270 ramifications that were fulfilled in one person, Jesus Christ.

"Jesus pointed to these prophecies on numerous occasions," I added, "to bolster His claims to be the Messiah, the Savior, the Son of God."

> Using the science of probability, we find the chances of just forty-eight of these prophecies being fulfilled in one person to be right at one in 10 to the 157th power.

> Furthermore, the task of matching up God's address with one man is further complicated by the fact that all the prophecies of the Messiah were made at least 400 years before He was to appear (209–214).

"That's all very interesting, but I still . . ."

"Wait, let me finish. In his book, McDowell continues by countering the possible argument that the fulfilled prophecy was merely coincidental."

H. Harold Artzler of the American Scientific Affiliation, in the foreword of a book by Peter W. Stoner writes:

> The manuscript for *Science Speaks* [regarding Jesus and fulfilled prophecy] has been carefully reviewed by a committee of the American Scientific Affiliation members and by the Executive Council of the same group and has been found, in general, to be dependable and accurate in regard to the scientific material presented. The mathematical analysis included is based

> upon principles of probability which are thoroughly sound, and Professor Stoner has applied these principles in a proper and convincing way.

"And here are Professor Stoner's findings about the probability of just eight of these prophecies being fulfilled in the one person of Jesus Christ. Remember, he's only talking about the probabilities of eight, not sixty, of these major prophecies occurring in one person."

> We find that the chance that any man might have lived down to the present time and fulfilled all eight prophecies is 1 in 10 to the 17th power.
>
> If we take 100,000,000,000,000,000 silver dollars and lay them on the face of Texas, they will cover all of the state two feet deep. Now mark one of these silver dollars and stir the whole mass thoroughly, all over the state. Blindfold a man and tell him that he can travel as far as he wishes, but he must pick up one silver dollar and say this is the right one. What chance would he have of getting the right one? Just the same chance that the prophets would have had of writing these eight prophecies and having them all come true in any one man, from their day to the present time, providing they wrote them in their own wisdom.
>
> Now these prophecies were either given by the inspiration of God or the prophets just wrote them as they thought they should be. In such a case the prophets had just one chance in 10 to the 17th power of having them come true in any man, but they all came true in Christ.
>
> This means that the fulfillment of these eight prophecies alone proves that God inspired the writing of these prophecies to a definiteness which lacks only one chance in 10 to the 17th power of being absolute.

"OK, those facts are quite compelling, but how can I be sure that what is written about Jesus in the Bible is true and not just mythological tales from the past?"

Ahh, the hook has been baited...

All too many people, like my young astrophysicist friend, have been raised believing that Christianity is just an emotion-based, crutch-like religion that is not substantiated by any facts at all. How thankful we can be for passages like Luke's preface to show us that we truly can fish with the facts to draw people towards the kingdom of God.

At the time of Luke's writing, many religions were competing for top spot in the Roman Empire. The world today has not changed much. The learned class was searching for trustworthy knowledge to guide them in their quest, as was my young friend. There was a need for fuller understanding on the part of both Theophilus and the astrophysicist. Some knowledge was in place but there was also a great possibility that hearsay facts or just plain misinformation was present.

Acts 28:22 shows that the Roman empire was not friendly towards Christianity, and rumors about Christians seemed to abound everywhere, much like today. "But we want to hear what your views are, for we know that people everywhere are talking against this sect [Christians]."

The need then and the need now hasn't changed. Both parties need the whole story. What makes Christianity the only way?

Luke makes it clear in 1:4 that he is writing to answer that very question—so that Theophilus may know the *certainty* of what he has been taught. Luke intends to show that what he writes is the real deal in order that transformation will occur in the life of the reader—then and now. The certainty of which Luke speaks is based upon **historical facts**.

In no other religion do we find the living God breaking into history seeking to save the lost. Definitive, historical facts are what separate Christianity from other religions that are merely based upon speculations, theories, or myths. The Christian faith has no need to hide from the facts.

The truth never hides from the light but rather seeks to have it shine even more brightly in order to affirm that which it teaches. Luke turns up the dimmer switch in order to assure his readers about the truthfulness of Jesus' life and teachings.

First, Luke shows the extreme care he takes as a historian in researching his work. He *carefully* investigated *everything* from the *beginning* in order to write an *orderly* account.

Luke spent time carefully investigating the multiple manuscripts and eyewitness accounts that told of the "things that have been fulfilled among us" (Luke 1:1) regarding the life and teachings of Jesus. He was not in a hurry to get some pabulum to press in order to be published. Luke desired to examine all the data available to him that he might give as detailed a picture as possible to those seeking the truth.

He traveled with the apostle Paul and learned firsthand from this eyewitness and others who had walked side-by-side with Jesus and could attest to His words and works. Throughout his travels, Luke sought to collect all the works written about Jesus he could find so that others might know the true story of Jesus from the beginning.

Secondly, Luke sought to assure his readers about the certainty of what they had been taught because it came from eyewitnesses such as Paul. His writings are the actual accounts of what happened, not fabrications or forgeries.

It is worth noting that Luke was writing at a time in history when the Gospel traditions were still being orally transmitted by apostolic witnesses! Because of that fact, Luke could not radically restructure the truth without his veracity being challenged. By necessity, his writings had to match fairly closely with the information that was being handed down through the rumor mill. The close relationship between his Gospel and the testimony of the eyewitnesses he alludes to in verse two simply supports his case. If Luke were going to deceive his readers, it would have been much wiser for him to have claimed to be an eyewitness himself.

As the apostle Paul attested to in Acts 26:25–26, "I am not insane, most excellent Festus," Paul replied. "What I am saying is true and reasonable. The king is familiar with these things, and I can speak freely to him. I am convinced that none of this has escaped his notice, because it was not done in a corner."

Or, as the apostle Peter stated, "We did not follow cleverly invented stories when we told you about the power and coming of our Lord Jesus Christ, but we were eyewitnesses of his majesty" (2 Peter 1:16).

The living voice of the apostles and other eyewitnesses of the Gospel story held the highest authority. However, as the Church continued to grow and expand its boundaries, and as the apostles died one by one, there came a need for another authoritative mode of transmitting the truth. Luke heard the call and wrote his gospel after much laborious research.

Lastly, Luke seeks in his prologue to assure his readers about the certainty of what they had been taught by pointing to Jesus' life as fulfilling the teachings of Scripture. These were prophecies that had been fulfilled in their midst.

Remember the odds of one man fulfilling just eight of the prophecies regarding the Messiah? Are you up for the silver dollar challenge?

Only one question remains for the seeker: "Even if I believe all that you've said, how do I know that what Luke originally wrote is the same thing we have in our hands? We don't have Luke's originals, so how do we know that what we have is authentic?"

The best response? Fish with the facts.

Josh McDowell does a fantastic job of addressing this issue through his own research and that of others. In summary:

> There are more than 5,300 known Greek manuscripts of the New Testament. Add over 10,000 Latin Vulgate and at least 9,300 other early versions and we have more

than 24,000 manuscript copies of portions of the New Testament in existence.

No other document of antiquity even begins to approach such numbers and attestation. In comparison, the Illiad by Homer is second with only 643 manuscripts that still survive.

Besides the number, the manuscripts of the New Testament differ from those of the classical authors, and this time the difference is clear gain. In no other case is the interval of time between composition of the book and the date of the earliest extant [existing] manuscripts so short as in that of the NT [Scraps, 25 years; whole sections, 250 years—compared to the Illiad, next closest at 500 years] (43–47).

Fishing Principle

Fish with the facts and let the world know who the One true God is. We, like the apostle Peter, do not follow cleverly invented stories when we tell others about the "power and coming of our Lord Jesus Christ" (2 Peter 1:16).

STUDY QUESTIONS

1. Have you ever read these facts about the messianic prophecies that were fulfilled by the life of Jesus? How do they make you feel about your decision to follow Jesus as a disciple? How do they make you feel about your commitment to the Great Commission? Take time to praise God for sending His Son into history that can be investigated. Pray for increased boldness in sharing these facts with those seeking the truth.

2. Discuss what the phrase blind faith means to you? Based on what you've read in this devotional, do you think this phrase can be appropriately applied to Christianity/disciples of Christ? Why or why not?

3. Have you ever had this type of encounter with an individual or group - people who believe in God but not that "Jesus is the only way to the Father?" Discuss what happened when your faith was challenged. How did you defend your faith? Would you do anything differently in the future?

4. Take time to read Psalm 1 and pray that it would become a reality in your life. Pray that the Holy Spirit will build in you a desire to know the historical facts of the faith in order to become more effective in fishing for those looking for the truth.

5. Is there anyone that you know that needs this type of bait to draw them towards Jesus? Take time to pray for this person, or people, that the Holy Spirit will prepare them to receive the truth. Pray that the Holy Spirit will give you the words to say and the proper attitude that those people might truly understand the facts of John 14:26 and 2 Peter 3:9.

Scripture

In the beginning was the Word, and the Word was with God, and the Word was God. He was with God in the beginning . . . The Word became flesh and lived for a while among us. We have seen his glory, the glory of the one and only Son, who came from the Father, full of grace and truth. (John 1:1–2,14)

Two

Fishing
Flesh *in the*

It was the end of a long journey.

The training, recuperating, and multiple competitions were behind them. Descending down the ramp, they boarded the plane with the boundless energy that only comes with youth. The belief was still intact: "We can do anything." The plane headed due east out of Los Angeles. The destination—Fort Sam Houston in San Antonio, Texas.

December 15, 1984, one coach and eight young men had come seeking to fulfill a dream. Soon these young men would be toeing the starting line in the hopes of capturing the Junior Olympic Cross Country National Championship.

For the uninitiated, high school cross country is a sport where runners traverse 3.1 miles of varied terrain (hopefully at high rates of speed) in an effort to reach the finish line ahead of their competitors. Each runner's final place is added together with his teammates' to determine the team's score. The team with the lowest score wins the competition. Hence, each runner carries an equal burden upon his shoulders.

I know, I can almost see you shaking your head at the very idea. But for this coach and eight 16-year-old young men, this was the mountain they had come to climb. Each of the young men hoped to be crowned the best in the nation; each also knew that his dream would only be a reality if the team ran as one.

The starting line stretched from one end of the field to the other. If you stood at one end, you could not even tell what colors the runners on the other end were brandishing. An eerie fog hung over the course making it impossible to tell which way the route veered a mere quarter of a mile from the start.

Some of the best high school runners in the United States paced about nervously as the frigid rain continued to descend. Their furrowed brows spoke volumes. One long strand of anxious athletes awaited the sound of the starter's pistol.

Seeing the heavy breathing and nervous twitches in his runners' bodies, the coach went over to say one last word of encouragement. "We've done the preparation, there's nothing more to do but run. We have what it takes to win it all. I'll be all over the course to encourage you, but I can't run for you. I believe in you!"

Turning to walk away, he overheard one of the runners say, "He really believes we can win!"

A lot of coaches use the word "we," but this was different. Never were any of these eight young men merely handed a workout as their coach idly sat by yelling out their times while eyeing a stopwatch. It wasn't a matter of photocopying the how-to's of the sport, the do's and the don'ts of distance running.

No, each one of these eight young men had run side-by-side with their coach throughout the year. He never asked them to do any workout that he wasn't willing to do. During the off-season he would run races with them to help them to see more clearly how to run a race. In the truest sense of the word, they were a team. These young men had seen their coach succeed, fatigue, sweat, tire, even fail. But they never saw him quit.

Every race they ran, he ran at least as many miles as they did, traversing a myriad of routes in order to see his runners at every imaginable—and unimaginable—point. Those times when the runners couldn't see him, they somehow still sensed his presence. He could not run in the flesh with his runners, but in spirit he was right beside them each step of the way.

And he would be there for them at the finish line, heart pounding, lungs searing. When they jettisoned down that final straightaway, the roar of the crowd was but an echo compared to the jubilation that enveloped his very soul—all in an effort to guide them to becoming accomplished runners.

The coach had a similar attitude to that modeled by Jesus in His own life. Jesus did not sit on high directing events. He came down into the filth of a barn to be born, to have most people misunderstand Him throughout His life, to end up on a cross, in order to cast the only net possible with which man could be saved. Jesus fished in the flesh.

Consider all Jesus gave up in order to show us the how-to's of running this race called life.

Jesus was there "in the beginning," before anything else. He was there before we humans began keeping track of time—before there was such a thing as finite time. Before any created thing came into being, Jesus was there.

And who was He with? God. Not only was Jesus there "in the beginning," but the phrase, "the Word was with God," shows us the intimate relationship He shares with the Father.

What was the source of this intimacy? "The Word [Jesus] was God." The mystery of Father and Son coexisting as one, with the Holy Spirit, was always a fact. The only way this is possible is for Jesus to be God.

The fact that Jesus "was in the beginning" means it will be a continual fact no matter what period in history we study the matter. "The Word [Jesus] was with God" means that from everlasting to everlasting the Father and Son are together. "The Word [Jesus] was God" means that He always has been, always will be. They are constants from the infinite to the finite and back again.

So why would Jesus choose to leave all of this to come down to earth in the flesh, to manifest Himself in a new form?

He submitted to the Father's plan in order that we, too, might reach the finish line. He gave it up for us. Jesus, "Who, being in very nature God, did not consider equality with God something to be grasped, but made himself nothing, taking the very nature of a servant, being made in human likeness. And being found in appearance as a man, he humbled himself and became obedient to death—even death on a cross" (Philippians 2:6–8).

It was the Father's plan that Jesus would share complete identification with mankind, without sinning, in order to help us see the glory and grace of the Father. He became visible that we might comprehend the invisible. He showed us that He was willing to do everything He asked us to do and more. "For God made Christ, who never sinned, to be the offering for our sin, so that we could be made right with God through Christ" (2 Cor. 5:21, NLT).

Jesus fished in the flesh that we might be able to run the race. In fact, He wanted us to be able to echo the words of the apostle Paul, "I have fought the good fight, I have finished the race, I have kept the faith" (2 Timothy 4:7).

It is apparent from the beginning of man's history that God never intended to simply give us a list of rules to live by and then disappear from the picture. Genesis 3:8 tells us, "Then the man and his wife heard the sound of the Lord God as he was walking in the garden in the cool of the day. . . ." What a beautiful picture of how it was meant to be—and how someday it will be again!

Even after man's sin barred him from the Garden of Eden, God was with His people. The form God chose was not as intimate, however, as when they were in the Garden. For example, before His people entered the Promised Land, God showed He was with the people in a unique way. "By day the Lord went ahead of them in a pillar of cloud to guide them on their way and by night in a pillar of fire to give them light, so that they could travel by day or night" (Exodus 13:21). Later, when the Israelites camped in the desert, God's presence (*shekinah*) encamped in the tabernacle, the tent of meeting. He was not an absentee landlord. He was present on the property.

God has always desired that His people know He is present. He has never been the God who created the world and stepped back to let it run its course. He has always sought to be intimately involved with His people. Hence, He went to the limit and sent His only Son, the Word incarnate—Jesus in the flesh. Our supreme example came out of our heavenly Father's desire to draw us home.

The "Word became flesh" and lived [literally, "pitched a tent, tabernacled"] among us. The same God who was with Israel in the tent of meeting, the tabernacle, chose to give up everything in order to "pitch a tent" with man—in the flesh. He fished in the flesh in order to help us see God, full of grace and truth. He walked with mankind to make visible the invisible.

Can we say the same in our attempts to reach out to the lost and lonely? Are we willing to run side-by-side with those who desperately need the Savior's touch?

Let's look at Peter and John who obviously were trained quite well in this particular fishing technique.

> One day Peter and John were going up to the temple at the time of prayer, three in the afternoon. Now a man crippled from birth was being carried to the temple gate called Beautiful, where he was put every day to beg from those going into the temple courts. When he saw Peter and John about to enter, he asked them for money. Peter looked straight at him, as did John. Then Peter said, "Look at us!" So the man gave them his attention, expecting to get something from them. Then Peter said, "Silver or gold I do not have, but what I have I give you. In the name of Jesus Christ of Nazareth, walk." Taking him by the right hand, he helped him up, and instantly the man's feet and ankles became strong. He jumped to his feet and began to walk..." (Acts 3:1–8a).

What did Peter and John immediately do after being asked for money? They looked "straight at him." What would be, or has been, our reaction in a similar situation? Do we look straight at the downtrodden seeking help? Or do we prefer to pretend we did not hear, or cross to the other side of the street where we know we will not be asked for help?

The apostles stopped, looked straight at the man, and then made sure he was paying attention to them: "Look at us!" With these three actions, Peter and John were expressing their deep feelings of compassion and empathy towards this man. Consider what that must have felt like for a man who regularly experienced other people looking away from him as if he did not exist.

Fishing in the flesh entails stopping and looking in order to see the inherent value in each person God places in our path in a day. We must seek the "imago dei," the image of God, in each person. We cannot walk by those in need (no matter what that need might be) as if we had not even seen them simply in an effort to alleviate our angst. Their needs might not be easily seen, but if we stop and look, who knows what we might find?

And who knows what power will come by God's grace through the human touch—the flesh? As Peter grasped the man's hand he was following his Teacher's frequent practice of making physical contact when healing a person.

People tend to listen when we are running alongside of them, when we can see and feel the rough terrain on which they are traversing. People would rather see a sermon than hear one.

Fishing Principle

Fish in the flesh. Stop, look, and listen. Look for the image of God in each encounter. Reach out your hand and ask, "What can I do for you?"

STUDY QUESTIONS

1. Have you ever had a teacher, coach, pastor, or friend exhibit this type of dedication toward you? Explain what that person did for you. How did it make you feel? Have you ever shown this type of dedication towards another person or group of people? What motivated you to do so? How did it make you feel?

2. Have you ever considered all that Jesus gave up in order to fish for us? Consider the gospel accounts and discuss what Jesus left behind, and what He went through, in order to come to earth for our salvation. Take time to praise Him for "fishing in the flesh" that we could live!

3. Discuss practical ways you can show the same attitude toward family members in order to fish for those who are lost. What are you willing to give up to show God's love? What do you have a "death grip" on that might be hindering such selfless expressions of love? Take time and pray that the Holy Spirit would open your eyes to see how you can help a family member join the race. Be open to changes He might be asking you to make.

4. Discuss how Jesus and His disciples showed compassion toward society's outcasts. Take time to pray that the Lord would give you that same type of compassion. Ask the Lord to show you the "unlovable" person or people He wants you to stop for, look at, and reach out your hand to.

5. Spend the next week practicing asking the question, "How are you?," and stopping to look and listen for the real answer. Practice reaching out your hand and asking, "What can I do for you?" Be ready to discuss the results at your next gathering. Pray for Joshua 1:9 to be a reality in this process - "Have I not commanded you? Be strong and courageous. Do not be terrified; do not be discouraged, for the Lord your God will be with you wherever you go."

Scripture

A record of the genealogy of Jesus Christ the son of David, the son of Abraham:

Abraham was the father of Isaac, Isaac the father of Jacob, Jacob the father of Judah and his brothers, Judah the father of Perez and Zerah, whose mother was Tamar, Perez the father of Hezron, Hezron the father of Ram, Ram the father of Amminadab, Amminadab the father of Nahshon, Nahshon the father of Salmon, Salmon the father of Boaz, whose mother was Rahab, Boaz the father of Obed, whose mother was Ruth, Obed the father of Jesse, and Jesse the father of King David.

David was the father of Solomon, whose mother had been Uriah's wife, Solomon the father of Rehoboam, Rehoboam the father of Abijah, Abijah the father of Asa, Asa the father of Jehoshaphat, Jehoshaphat the father of Joram, Joram the father of Uzziah, Uzziah the father of Jotham, Jotham the father of Ahaz, Ahaz the father of Hezekiah, Hezekiah the father of Manasseh, Manasseh the father of Amon, Amon the father of Josiah, and Josiah the father of Jeconiah and his brothers at the time of the exile to Babylon.

After the exile to Babylon: Jeconiah was the father of Shealtiel, Shealtiel the father of Zerubbabel, Zerubbabel the father of Abiud, Abiud the father of Eliakim, Eliakim the father of Azor, Azor the father of Zadok, Zadok the father of Akim, Akim the father of Eliud, Eliud the father of Eleazar, Eleazar the father of Matthan, Matthan the father of Jacob, and Jacob the father of Joseph, the husband of Mary, of whom was born Jesus, who is called Christ (Matthew 1:1-16).

Three

Fishing
with
Grace

Okay, be honest now. How many of you read that genealogy? Skimmed it? Skipped it altogether?

I know, I know. You're probably thinking, "Why bother reading a cumbersome list of names? What's the point? I thought this book was about fishing techniques used by Jesus and the disciples. What good can a person possibly glean from Jesus' genealogy?"

I asked these same questions for many years and would simply skip down to verse 18 where the good part begins. But one day the Holy Spirit prompted me to take seriously the words of 2 Timothy 3:16–17:

"All Scripture is inspired by God and is useful to teach us what is true and to make us realize what is wrong in our lives. It straightens us out and teaches us to do what is right. It is God's way of preparing us in every way, fully equipped for every good thing God wants us to do" (NLT).

"Tell me Holy Spirit," I asked, "what possible preparation to do Your work can I receive from this genealogy?"

Come along with me and I'll share with you lessons that were laid upon my heart from this simple list of names, lessons that have helped me to understand one of the ways our Lord wants us to fish.

As I pondered the possible value of a list of names I wondered, "What would it be like if my name were included on that list? Would I so blithely cast it aside as of little value? Or, would I cherish my inclusion?"

Ever been to a school graduation ceremony? What's the first thing you did when you received that printed list of names of all the graduates? Did you search for the name or names of loved ones, family or friends? How would you feel if those names were left off the list?

Genealogies in God's Word are no different! These are real people with real stories created in the image of God.

In fact, genealogies were the most natural way for Jews to begin the story of a man's life. This fact alone helped me to appreciate again that Christianity is rooted in history (see Chapter 1, "Fishing with the Facts") and not mere mythology like what is found in Buddhism and Hinduism, for example.

Perhaps if I looked more closely at these ancestors of the Anointed One, I would find some graduation stories of a different sort—something that would help me to become a better fisherman. Let's look together.

A careful reading of this genealogy reveals something that differs markedly from stereotypical Jewish genealogies: women are listed. Women had no legal rights in that culture. They were regarded as little more than property by most.

Why would Jesus' genealogy take a radical departure from the norm and list women—Tamar, Rahab, Ruth, and Uriah's wife? And, why these women? Why not the famous faithful—Sarah, Rebecca, and Rachel?

Tamar, Rahab, Ruth, and Bathsheba? Hardly the women of virtue that we humans would choose to mention in the lineage of the Lion of Judah, the King of Kings and Lord of Lords.

In Genesis 38 we read the story of Tamar and her father-in-law Judah. When Tamar's husband died, it was the responsibility of her oldest brother-in-law to marry her in order to continue on the name of her husband (Levirate marriage commanded in Deuteronomy 25:5–6).

Judah told his son, Onan, to fulfill his duty to produce offspring for his brother: "You must marry Tamar, as our law requires of the brother of a man who has died. Her first son from you will be your brother's heir" (Genesis 38:8, NLT). Onan refused so the Lord took Onan's life.

Judah, fearing for the life of his youngest son, told Tamar to go back to her father's house. She was to remain a widow until Judah's youngest son, Shelah, was old enough to marry her.

However, it became obvious as time went on that Judah had no intention of having Shelah fulfill his obligation: "But Judah didn't really intend to do this because he was afraid Shelah would also die, like his two brothers" (Genesis 38:11b, NLT).

So what does Tamar do to make sure that she is taken care of, that the commands of the Levirate marriage are fulfilled? Go to Yahweh in prayer? Confront her father-in-law? Seek help from extended family members?

NO! She disguises herself as a prostitute, and Judah, her father-in-law, unknowingly sleeps with her. From this incestuous/adulterous relationship comes Perez and Zerah—some of Jesus' ancestors!

Would you choose Tamar to be part of the Lord's line?

And what of Rahab? We read in Joshua 2 that, "Joshua son of Nun secretly sent two spies from Shittim. 'Go, look over the land,' he said, 'especially Jericho.' So they went and entered the house of a prostitute named Rahab and stayed there" (v. 1).

A prostitute and a non-Jew. Need any more be said?

Speaking of non-Jews, how did Ruth ever get included in this list? She was a Moabitess—a nation that historically was a bitter enemy of Israel. Moab was a nation born of incestuous relations between Lot and his daughters when they got him drunk and lay with him (Genesis 19:30–38).

Is anybody else seeing a pattern here?

Moab—a nation so detested that Deuteronomy 23:3 says that, "No Ammonite or Moabite or any of his descendants may enter the assembly of the Lord, even down to the tenth generation." Moabites were not allowed into the assembly of the Lord—and yet Ruth ended up in the Lord's family tree?

And who can forget Bathsheba? "Wait a minute," you say, "I don't see Bathsheba listed anywhere!" Look closely at verse 6 which lists Solomon's mother as "Uriah's wife." Remember the story now?

We read in 2 Samuel 11 that David was hanging out on his palace roof and spotted a woman over on the next rooftop taking a bath. Rather than avert his eyes to the sight, David sent someone to find out who the beautiful woman was.

Word returned that she was the wife of Uriah the Hittite. But this didn't stop David from sending messengers to get her. "She came to him, and he slept with her" (2 Samuel 11:4). Apparently Bathsheba was all-too-willing to acquiesce to the King's call.

The result? Bathsheba became pregnant by an adulterous liaison with David. David tried to trick Uriah into sleeping with Bathsheba, but to no avail. So in order to cover up what happened, David had Uriah killed in battle.

David then married Bathsheba but their firstborn son died. From this union, however, eventually came the next king, Solomon, and eventually the King who reigns forever.

Whew! The sordid array of events involving these four women eventually lead to the birth of Jesus.

Who in their right mind would include these women in Jesus' genealogy? Three of the women were non-Jews, which makes a pure pedigree impossible. Gentiles, indeed! Why everyone knows they're unclean from birth.

Three of them were suspected of adultery! The possible penalty for such a sin was death: "If a man commits adultery with another man's wife, both the man and the woman must be put to death" (Leviticus 20:10, NLT).

Jesus could have been linked to a pure and unstained background, free from any whispers behind the back, any hint of scandal. But He chose not to. Why?

This, my beloved, is a genealogy of GRACE, a lineage of love. Christ chose to be made in the likeness of sinful flesh. "Though he was God, he did not demand and cling to his rights as God. He made himself nothing, he took the humble position of a slave and appeared in human form" (Philippians 2:7–8, NLT).

From the beginning, Jesus chose to have His life history as a man traced through Gentiles as well as Jews, men as well as women, sinners as well as saints.

God's covenant with Abraham in Genesis 12 told of a nation coming forth from his descendants that would be a blessing unto all nations. This covenant culminated in Jesus' Great Commission found in Matthew 28 proving that it is not God's desire that anyone should perish. "He is patient with you, not wanting anyone to perish, but everyone to come to repentance" (2 Peter 3:9).

All the descendants were not Jewish. This was a reminder to the Jews that they alone were not the only ones loved by God—a rebuke of Jewish pride and their well-known hatred of Gentiles. Claiming descent from Abraham (or, today, any "godly" founding family of a church, or pride in a denomination or movement) insures nothing, except boasting in the flesh.

> This is what the Lord says:
> "Let not the wise man boast of his wisdom
> or the strong man boast of his strength

or the rich man boast of his riches,
but let him who boasts boast about this:
that he understands and knows me, that I am the
    Lord, who exercises kindness,
justice and righteousness on earth,
for in these I delight," declares the Lord.
"The days are coming," declares the Lord, "when I will
    punish all who are circumcised only in the
    flesh . . ."
(Jeremiah 9:23–25).

Salvation comes not from man, but from God. "God saved you by his special favor [grace] when you believed. And you can't take credit for this; it is a gift from God. Salvation is not a reward for the good things we have done, so none of us can boast about it" (Ephesians 2:8–9, NLT).

Jesus came to be a Savior to the entire world, not select subgroups. Pointing to anyone or anything other than Jesus is akin to idolatry.

All the descendants were not men. Inclusion of the four women was a unique way of affirming the value of women. When God created man, "He created man in His own image, in the image of God he create him, male and female He created them" (Genesis 1:27). Women are highly valued in God's economy. They are not considered second-class citizens.

All the descendants were sinners. Even the best of them had checkered points along their paths. None were able to stand innocent before the judgment seat of their own accord, not even the "Fathers of the Faith." Not Abraham, not Isaac, not Jacob, nor even the great King David, the man who sought after God's own heart, were able to stand blameless.

Twice we find Abraham lying about his relationship with Sarah because he feels a need to protect himself rather than rely upon the Lord's promises (Genesis 12:10–20; Genesis 20). Furthermore, in Genesis 16:1–6, Abraham acquiesces to Sarah's plan to circumvent God's promise of an offspring to them. She tells Abraham to sleep with her handmaiden Hagar. These sinful actions come from the man of whom it is said, "It was by faith that Sarah together with Abraham was able to have a child, even though they were too old and Sarah was barren. Abraham believed that God would keep his promise" (Hebrews 11:11).

It seems that Isaac learned the art of deception from his Dad when it came to potentially dangerous situations with his wife in foreign lands. The story in Genesis 26:1–11 is a virtual mirror of Abraham's deceptive practices in Genesis 12 and 20.

And who can forget the story of Jacob deceiving his brother Esau out of his birthright in Genesis 25:27–34. The very name Jacob can figuratively mean "he deceives." Jacob does a good job trying to live up to this moniker by stealing his brother's blessing also. "Esau said, 'Isn't he rightly named Jacob? He has deceived me these two times: He took my birthright, and now he's taken my blessing!'" (Genesis 27:36).

The perfect patriarchs? Hardly.

What about the persons you want to share the Good News with? What sins do they deem so dastardly that no one could ever forgive them?

Help them to see that their names can be written in the greatest list of all—the everlasting book of life!

Fishing Principle

Fish with grace. Show those who believe they are unlovable how God's grace has worked in your life and the lives of men and women throughout Scripture. Remember, "He came not to call the righteous, but sinners" (Matthew 9:13).

STUDY QUESTIONS

1. Did you read every name in Jesus' genealogy? Why or why not? What do the genealogies sprinkled throughout Scripture tell you about God's concern for individual people? Are there any meaningless names in Scripture? What would it be like if your name was not written in the Everlasting Book of Life? What if the names of your family or friends were missing?

2. What does Jesus' genealogy do when responding to those who say that "Christianity belittles the value of women"? How can you effectively use this genealogy to fish for people who think this way?

3. Carefully read Genesis 38, Joshua 2, and 2 Samuel 11. Visualize yourself in the roles of Tamar, Rahab, and Bathsheba. Take time to praise God for His grace that allowed these women, and Ruth, to be a part of the Lord's lineage. Take time to praise God for allowing you to become part of His family through grace upon grace.

4. Read and dwell on the following statements and discuss the implications for you today: "All the ancestors of Jesus were not Jewish"; "All the ancestors of Jesus were not men"; "All the ancestors of Jesus were sinners." Take time to pray that the Holy Spirit would reveal any ways in which your attitude may have sought to make your brand of Christianity exclusive. Ask forgiveness for any revealed sinful desire or actions that have cause you to stray from seeking to fulfill the Great Commission.

5. Take time to dwell on Acts 1:8 and ask the Holy Spirit to grant that you might play your part. Ask the Holy Spirit to lay on your heart those you know who believe they are unlovable. Share these names with each other and pray that you might be Jesus' hands in extending His grace.

Scripture

In the sixth month {of the pregnancy of Eliza-beth—soon to be mom of John the Baptist}, God sent the angel Gabriel to Nazareth, a town in Galilee, to a virgin pledged to be married to a man named Joseph, a descendant of David. The virgin's name was Mary. The angel went to her and said, "Greetings, you who are highly fa-vored! The Lord is with you."

Mary was greatly troubled at his words and wondered what kind of greeting this might be. But the angel said to her, "Do not be afraid, Mary, you have found favor with God. You will be with child and give birth to a son, and you are to give him the name Jesus. He will be great and will be called the Son of the Most High. The Lord God will give him the throne of his father David, and he will reign over the house of Jacob forever; his kingdom will never end."

"How will this be," Mary asked the angel, "since I am a virgin?"

The angel answered, "The Holy Spirit will come upon you, and the power of the Most High will overshadow you. So the holy one to be born will be called the Son of God. Even Elizabeth your relative is going to have a child in her old age, and she who was said to be barren is in her sixth month. For nothing is impossible with God."

"I am the Lord's servant," Mary answered. "May it be to me as you have said." Then the angel left her.
(Luke 1:26-38)

Four

Fishing *with* Mom

Mom! The very word used to be pregnant with positive portraits of women nurturing their infants and toddlers. Women believed they were called of God to this majestic position—molders of mankind.

In recent decades, however, moms have often been made to feel incomplete if they didn't work outside the home. Stay-at-home moms have been barraged with messages from the world that chides them as losers in women's search for significance; pawns in man's attempt to keep women from equality!

Which is it? Pawns of men or molders of mankind?

The first sound that a fetus hears is mom's heart. The first voice it registers as a known is mom's—talking, singing, reading, praying, and blessing. Mom's hands are the first ones that cuddle the infant and make him or her feel safe in the loud, bright world. Mom is the first one, to feed the little one from her own body.

A connection created by God—mom and infant.

And during those early years, it is mom's reassuring voice that constantly conveys God's love. There is no greater influence in the home when young eyes are seeing things for the first time, when the mind is comprehending the world for the first time, when the tongue is forming words for the first time, when the body is learning how to move in harmony for the first time.

Mom is it!

For all too many mothers and children, in America at least, it is no longer like this. Babies in the womb are hearing annual reports, stockholders' meetings, and *Wall Street Weekly* more than the Word.

For a myriad of reasons, from truly needing a second income to overextended finances to single motherhood due to the disintegration of the American family, moms are back at the job within eight weeks after their babies are born.

The great influencer now becomes day care for many a child. How many moms are now missing those firsts? The first word, the first laugh, the first step, the first fall. And no matter how good a day care is, it can never replace what God intended—MOM.

Jesus' mom knew that. She was steeped in Scripture that compared the love of God for His people to the love of a mom for her child. Out of every comparison in the world that God could have chosen to express His love, He chose that of a mom for her child:

> "Yet Jerusalem says, 'The Lord has deserted us; the Lord has forgotten us.' 'Never! Can a mother forget her nursing child? Can she feel no love for a child she has borne?" (Isaiah 49:14–15, NLT).

> "Rejoice with Jerusalem! Be glad with her, all you who love her and mourn for her. Delight in Jerusalem! Drink deeply of her glory even as an infant drinks at its mother's generous breasts. Peace and prosperity will overflow Jerusalem like a river,' says the Lord. 'The wealth of the nations will flow to her. Her children will be nursed at her breasts, carried in her arms, and treated with love. I will comfort you there as a child is comforted by its mother" (Isaiah 66:10–13, NLT).

For Mary, an Israelite woman, her primary role was to be a mom and nurture her children. To be a mom was the most highly coveted role an Israelite woman could fulfill. There was no higher calling. Conversely, to be a childless woman was a painful lot in the Israelite culture, as can be seen by the stories of Sarah, Rachel, and Elizabeth, for example.

Mary was spared such agony when God chose her to be the mother of the Messiah. But did she truly have a molding influence on Jesus' life, the God-man? Did His years as an infant and toddler at His mother's knee impact who He became? Did Joseph ever roll his eyes at Mary when she said, "I wonder where He learned that?"

We can learn a great deal about Mary's influence on Jesus' development from the first chapter of Luke. First, we witness her **humility**.

Verse 28 states, "The angel went to her and said, 'Greetings, you who are highly favored! The Lord is with you." Mary's response? "She was greatly troubled at his words and wondered what kind of greeting this might be" (vs. 29).

She was a lowly peasant girl from Galilee. Two strikes against her in the eyes of the world. When are the poor ever considered "highly favored"? And as for Galileans, they were considered inferior by the Jews in Jerusalem.

The Sanhedrin [the ruling body of Judaism] sat in Jerusalem so that city was considered the center of all knowledge. Hence, the Galileans did not have the luxury of learning from these oft-times sanctimonious sages.

The thought of the Messiah being raised in Galilee was preposterous to the elitist living in Jerusalem. "Nazareth! [a town in the region of Galilee] Can anything good come from there?" (John 1:46). Impossible! How could the Lion of Judah be raised by such country bumpkins?

All these thoughts must have flooded Mary's mind as she considered the "highly favored" moniker. She knew she didn't deserve such a greeting. Her meritorious lifestyle promised no such reward. That is why she was "greatly troubled." This greeting made no sense in Mary's frame of reference.

49

Isn't this the same frame of reference we see in Jesus' lifestyle and teaching?

Did He come into the world claiming a crown, a carriage, and a castle? Did He look down upon the ill-cultured, illiterate, poor Galileans? Did He spend His time pointing to Himself, or pointing to His Father? Jesus' humanity learned well, and taught well, the tenets of humility learned from His mother's example.

Secondly, we witness Mary's **courage** and **conviction**.

"How will this be," Mary asked the angel, "since I am a virgin?" (v. 34).

Mary was betrothed, pledged to be married, to Joseph. She didn't comprehend how this promise from Gabriel was to play out in the present situation.

A betrothal, or engagement, in biblical times differed significantly from today. Mary and Joseph would have made an oral commitment in the presence of witnesses and sealed it with a pledge—a piece of money or a written agreement. It was almost as binding as marriage itself and could only be dissolved through a formal divorce. From the moment of the betrothal on, Mary and Joseph would have been referred to as "husband and wife."

The relationship would now be considered sacred, binding in God's eyes. However, months might pass before the actual wedding might occur. Sexual relations with Joseph, therefore, were inconceivable. So how was this pregnancy to occur?

"The Holy Spirit will come upon you, and the power of the Most High will overshadow you" (v. 35). Having the Holy Spirit as the agent of impregnation still left Mary with a predicament. If she became pregnant before her marriage to Joseph had been consummated she could be subject to death by stoning (Deuteronomy 22:23–24) as a worst-case scenario. At best, there would be whispers behind her back, or open criticism and ridicule.

Her response? Mary was willing to lose Joseph and even face the possibility of stoning in order to be obedient to God.

"I am the Lord's servant," Mary answered. "May it be to me as you have said" (v. 38).

Was this not the same courage we see exhibited by Jesus as He enters Jerusalem for the last time? He knows what lies ahead, and yet He moves forward obediently.

Sounds hauntingly familiar doesn't it? Remember Jesus' prayer upon the Mount of Olives? "Father, if you are willing, take this cup from me; yet not my will but your will be done" (John 22:42). The courage of a mother passed on to her child?

Thirdly, we see Mary's **knowledge of Scripture.**

Upon finding out about Mary's resolve to believe the angel's message, Elizabeth [Mary's cousin] says, "Blessed is she [Mary] who has believed that what the Lord has said to her will be accomplished!" (Luke 1:45).

Mary responds with a song of praise unto the Lord:

My soul praises the Lord
and my spirit rejoices in God my Savior,
for he has been mindful
of the humble state of his servant.
From now on all generations will call me blessed,
for the Mighty One has done great things for me—
holy is his name.
His mercy extends to those who fear him,
from generation to generation.
He has performed mighty deeds with his arm;
he has scattered those who are proud in their
inmost thoughts.
He has brought down rulers from their thrones
but has lifted up the humble.
He has filled the hungry with good things
but has sent the rich away empty.
He has helped his servant Israel,
remembering to be merciful
to Abraham and his descendants forever,
even as he said to our fathers. (Luke 1:46–55)

It is within this song that we understand that Mary's life has been steeped in Scripture. She didn't sit down and compose a medley upon hearing Elizabeth's encouragement. No, the majority of these words come directly from the Tanakh (Jewish Scriptures—our Old Testament). Her heart wells up with the Words of God she has written upon her heart.

Any wonder where Jesus was taught these Scriptures that He knew so well and used so artistically on His fishing trips?

Fishing Principle

Pray about priorities. Fish for your children with humility, conviction, and God's Word. Moms can positively influence the next generation of fisherman and fisherwomen, if they so choose.

STUDY QUESTIONS

1. Do you believe that moms have the greatest human influence on their young children's lives? Why or why not? What has caused many moms to seek their value/ significance outside of the home? How do you feel about this? In the last five years, more moms are leaving the workforce than ever before in order to work just at home. Why do you think this is occurring?

2. Take time to pray about your current work situation - be it at home or outside the home and home combined. Pray for spouses and friends who are moms. Realize that neither situation is inherently right or wrong. Pray that the Holy Spirit would guide you, or your spouse, and friends to be the best moms possible. Ask the Holy Spirit to reveal if there are any definitive changes that need to occur so our children are being trained and equipped in the best environment possible.

3. Look at Mary's life and discuss how much influence a mom can have in the spiritual development of her young children. Discuss specific examples of humility seen in Jesus' life. Discuss specific examples of courage and conviction in Jesus' life. Discuss specific examples of Jesus' use of Scripture in His life. Remember, Jesus was fully man as well as fully God. A mystery yes, but He learned at His mom's knee.

4. Search the Scriptures and discuss any other biblical moms who influenced their children - positively and negatively. Take time to pray that God would transform you, or a mom you know, to become more like the positive biblical moms you know. Pray that the Holy Spirit would quicken moms' spirits when they begin drifting towards the negative models so they can get back on the proper path (Psalm 119:105).

5. Meditate and pray upon Acts 1:8 and visualize your children/family as being your Jerusalem - the first people where moms are to be witnesses for Jesus. Read, discuss, and pray about Deuteronomy 6 and the implications it has in moms' fishing for children.

Scripture

This is how the birth of Jesus came about. His mother Mary was pledged to be married to Joseph, but before they came together, she was found to be with child through the Holy Spirit. Because Joseph her husband was a righteous man and did not want to expose her to public disgrace, he had in mind to divorce her quietly.

But after he had considered this, an angel of the Lord appeared to him in a dream and said, "Joseph son of David, do not be afraid to take Mary home as your wife, because what is conceived in her is from the Holy Spirit. She will give birth to a son, and you are to give him the name Jesus, because he will save his people from their sins."

All this took place to fulfill what the Lord had said through the prophet: "The virgin will be with child and will give birth to a son, and they will call him Immanuel"—which means, "God with us."

When Joseph woke up, he did what the angel of the Lord had commanded him and took Mary home as his wife. But he had no union with her until she gave birth to a son. And he gave him the name Jesus. (Matthew 1:18–25)

Five

Fishing with Dad

Dad. Who better to teach a son how to fish? Dad comes into the bedroom before the sun even thinks of rising. "Time to get up, Slugger," he whispers. Muffled sounds arise from under the covers...Tick...Tick...Tick...

Five minutes later the scene is reenacted with a gentle jostling of a leg peeking out from under the covers. "What Dad?!!!"

"It's Saturday, Buddy. Remember? I'm going to teach you how to fish—just you and me."

Covers catapult into the air. Slugger is in full motion. A new land speed record is set for changing from pajamas into fishing clothes—so what if the socks don't match and the shoes are on the wrong feet.

With a tug on the bill of his cap, Slugger is out the bedroom door, bounding down the stairs hitting every third one. "Ah, just me and dad."

As they pull slowly out of the driveway, there is almost no need for headlights. Slugger's smile is beaming so brightly it's almost blinding.

The tips of the poles are dangling over the back seat, bobbers and fish hooks dancing in the air. Dad's right arm is laying across the front seat, hand firmly on his son's shoulder.

It's a scene from Norman Rockwell.

Unfortunately, all too many boys in America never experience this type of camaraderie with their dads. A chance to learn one-on-one from the man they hold up as The Master never comes. Why?

Absentee fathers litter the landscape in America for a multitude of reasons: divorce, never married moms, "too busy," or lack of proper priorities. One of the results? Jails in America are overcrowded with fatherless boys. And resentment towards dad for the neglect is at an apex.

Consider the following condensed version of a story I heard on the radio not too long ago.

One year at Mother's Day a greeting card company decided to donate cards to a Federal Penitentiary. The company thought it would a nice way for the prisoners to connect with their moms. The turnout for prisoners desiring cards was staggering. Prisoners waiting in line far outnumbered the supply of cards. In response, the card company promised to return with more cards so every prisoner who wanted to send one would get one.

The Mother's Day card giveaway being such a success, the card company decided to do the same thing for Father's Day. Not wanting a reoccurrence of the Mother's Day problem, the company brought a surplus. The result? Almost every box was carted back to the company—unopened. Only a handful of prisoners desired to send a card to their dads. Pretty telling, huh?

The person who should have the greatest positive impact on a son's life apparently is all-too-often nowhere to be found.

This dilemma isn't merely the problem of those families whose sons have ended up in jail. No, a whole generation of latchkey kids from families, even Christian ones, haven't been learning how to fish from their fathers, either. Who's going to teach them?

Perhaps a little bumper sticker theology will answer that question: "If you don't teach your kids about wildlife, someone else will!"

Sunday schools, youth groups, and Christian schools aren't the answer. These are supposed to supplement what's taught at home, not be the primary mode of modeling proper fishing techniques.

If you're still not convinced this dilemma can happen, and is happening, in Christian homes today, perhaps a glimpse at King David's parenting practices will change your mind.

Remember David, the "man after God's own heart?" Certainly he taught his children how to be witnesses to the world about Yahweh and His promises to bless all nations through Abraham (cf. Genesis 12). Certainly he taught them proper fishing techniques through his own example—didn't he?

Not according to the events recorded in 2 Samuel 13:

David's oldest son was Amnon, whose mom was Ahinoam. David's third born son was Absalom. He and his sister, Tamar, had Maacah for their mom.

Well it seems that,

> In the course of time, Amnon son of David fell in love with Tamar, the beautiful sister of Absalom son of David.
>
> Amnon became frustrated to the point of illness on account of his sister Tamar, for she was a virgin, and it seemed impossible for him to do anything to her (verses 1–2).

Amnon, with the help of his cousin Jonadab, cooked up a plot to alleviate his frustrations. Rather than dealing with a problem according to Scriptural tenets, Amnon decided that he deserved to be fulfilled. Sound familiar? David on a rooftop, Bathsheba in a bathtub?

Amnon put his plan into action,

> So Amnon lay down and pretended to be ill. When the king came to see him, Amnon said to him, "I would like my sister Tamar to come and make some bread in my sight, so I may eat from her hand. . . ."

> Then Amnon said to Tamar, "Bring the food here into my bedroom so I may eat from your hand" . . . But when she took it to him to eat, he grabbed her and said, "Come to bed with me, my sister."
>
> "Don't my brother!" she said to him. "Don't force me. Such a thing should not be done in Israel! . . ." But he refused to listen to her, and since he was stronger than she, he raped her" (verses 6,10–14).

David's response? "When King David heard all this, he was furious" (vs. 21). That's it! He was furious—so what? Where's the discipline, the punishment, the teaching, the fishing lesson for the future?

There is no record anywhere that David did anything besides being "furious." What kind of an example is this? David abdicated his responsibility as a dad. And this lack of leadership eventually led to the death of Amnon, and to the attempts by Absalom, and later Adonijah, to usurp their father David from the throne by seeking his very life!

Still think it can't happen in Christian homes today? Dads, have you taken your kids fishing lately?

Fortunately, Christian men in America have been receiving a wake up call of late. Whatever you may think of the Promise Keepers movement, it is accomplishing one thing for certain—men are hearing an alarm.

A chance to learn how to fish from surrogate dads is being offered to those who never learned, or those who, like Slugger, forgot about the importance of Saturday morning.

For some, the offer falls upon deaf ears—spiritual slumber continues...Tick...Tick...Tick. Other men are still making muffled sounds upon having their hibernation hindered. "Just five more minutes," and the snooze button is tapped again.

But, there is a final group that is creating a virtual vortex by their spinning and whirling as they search frantically for long forgotten fishing clothes. There is a distant memory of a call to be a role model, to be an example, that will draw children towards the Lord so they too may be propelled forth to do the same for others.

Oh that our children may take part in the greatest fishing trip ever being assembled:

> Jesus came and told his disciples, "I have been given complete authority in heaven and on earth. Therefore, go and make disciples of all the nations, baptizing them in the name of the Father and the Son and the Holy Spirit. Teach these new disciples to obey all the commands I have given you. And be sure of this: I am with you always, even to the end of the age" (Matthew 28:18–20).

That bright light that comes from a smile. It comes from dads, too. Watching a son bait the hook attempting to imitate the precision he saw from dad; watching a son holding his rod just the same way he pictured dad doing it; watching a son cast the line out upon the water and get in the exact same crouch as dad to keep an eye on that bobber; watching eyes bulge, knuckles whiten, and reels spin as the first catch is a moment away.

What about Mary's husband? Did Joseph have any positive influence on the development of Jesus? Did the King of Kings and Lord of Lords learn anything about fishing for men from Joseph?

Probably. Little is known about this carpenter from Nazareth. But what we do know speaks volumes about the fact that "children learn by what is caught as well as by what is taught."

Joseph would have understood the call to be a positive example as a dad. Since childhood, he would most likely would have daily recited the Shema,

> Hear, O Israel: The Lord our God, the Lord is one. Love the Lord your God with all your heart, and with all your soul and with all your strength. These commandments that I give you today are to be upon your hearts. Impress them on your children. Talk about them when you sit at home and when you walk along the road, when you lie down and when you get up" (Deuteronomy 6:5–7).

Can't you just picture father and son standing over a table at the carpenter's shop discussing the Law and life. Yep, Joseph was a dad. An adoptive one, yes, but he was nevertheless a dad. A dad who sought to model the craft of a carpenter and the character of a King.

And he did it from the very moment Jesus was conceived by the Holy Spirit in Mary.

First we witness Joseph's **righteousness** (verse 19). When Joseph discovers that Mary is pregnant, there is only one recourse in his mind: divorce. How could he possibly know the cause of Mary's conception? The natural conclusion was that Mary had been unfaithful, she had broken her pledge.

Joseph was a man of conviction that desired with his whole heart to follow God's law. God took the marriage vow seriously, hence, so did Joseph. Jewish laws typically required a husband to divorce a wife in cases of adultery. A holy man, one seeking to be obedient to God's commandments, couldn't even think of consummating his marriage.

The woman he loved and was betrothed to. God he loved and was committed to. Joseph placed service to God above his own heartfelt desires toward his wife.

It's hard not to hear the strains of Jesus own voice, "Anyone who loves his father or mother more than me is not worthy of me; anyone who loves his son or daughter [husband or wife] more than me is not worthy of me" (Matthew 10:37).

Secondly, we witness Joseph's **compassion** (verse 19).

Yes, as a righteous man Joseph believed that divorce was his only option. But simultaneously he must have felt that sword piercing his heart. He loved Mary. She was the woman he longed to be with.

Accordingly, Joseph chose to divorce Mary quietly. An out-of-court settlement would be best. He didn't want Mary to face the possibility of public disgrace and scorn. And he certainly didn't want to see her face the ultimate penalty permitted by law, death by stoning. Joseph would divorce her without specifying the reason. He loved this woman and had compassion on her.

Sounds like Jesus, doesn't it?

> The teachers of the law and the Pharisees brought in a woman caught in adultery. They made her stand before the group and said to Jesus, "Teacher, this woman was caught in the act of adultery. In the Law, Moses commanded us to stone such women. Now what do you say?" They were using this question as a trap, in order to have a basis for accusing him.
>
> But Jesus bent down and started to write on the ground with his finger. When they kept on questioning him, he straightened up and said to them, "If any one of you is without sin, let him be the first to throw a stone at her." Again he stooped down and wrote on the ground.
>
> At this, those who heard began to go away one at a time, the older ones first, until only Jesus was left, with the woman still standing there. Jesus straightened up and asked her, "Woman, where are they? Has no one condemned you?"
>
> "No one, sir," she said.
>
> "Then neither do I condemn you," Jesus declared. "Go now and leave your life of sin." (John 8:3–11).

Thirdly, we witness Joseph's **pondering** (verse 20).

He loved this woman, believed he knew the proper thing to do, and yet he "considered" the situation carefully. He didn't act hastily. He "had in his mind to divorce her quietly" and yet he delayed. A decision of this magnitude had to be pondered in the "spirit of the law versus letter of the law."

Remember the woman caught in adultery. According to the Law of Moses, wasn't the proper thing to do obvious? Rather than answer immediately, what do we see Jesus do?

63

"But Jesus bent down and started to write on the ground with his finger" (John 8:6). Pondering the possibilities?

Fourthly, we see Joseph's **obedience** (v. 24).

Joseph's plans to divorce Mary are radically restructured after an angel appears to him in a dream. The baby is conceived by the Holy Spirit! There is no need for a divorce!

Does Joseph question? No. "When Joseph woke up, he did what the angel of the Lord had commanded him and took Mary home as his wife" (Matthew 1:24).

Joseph was doing God's will—the one thing he desired to do from the start. In the process he was allowed to provide protection and love for the mother of his Lord, and serve God's son as a surrogate dad.

> Sing praises to God and to his name!
> Sing loud praises to him who rides the clouds.
> His name is the Lord—
> rejoice in his presence!
> Father to the fatherless, defender of widows—
> this is God, whose dwelling is holy (Psalm 68:4–5).

Jesus was doing His Father's will—the one thing he wanted to do from the start and to the finish.

> "Abba, Father," he [Jesus] said, "everything is possible for you. Take this cup from me. Yet not what I will, but what you will" (Mark. 14:36).

Fishing Principle

Tick...Tick...Tick...Sons and daughters need an example of how to fish: righteousness, compassion, prayerful pondering, obedience. For some the role may be father to the fatherless.

STUDY QUESTIONS

1. Do you think it's overstating the case to say that, "Dads should be the greatest single positive impact on their sons' lives as they grow from toddler to teens...and beyond?" Discuss why or why not. How do you think men in America, as a group, are doing in this area? Remember, "If you don't teach your kids about wildlife, someone else will."

2. Take time to praise God for the Promise Keeper's movement, and other similar movements, that are helping dads to turn their hearts back toward home. If you do not have any specific training for dads in your local congregation/area, pray that the Holy Spirit would raise up leaders, funding, and material for such ventures.

3. How much positive influence can a dad really have in the spiritual development of his sons (and daughters)? Joseph was a man of righteousness and conviction - discuss specific examples where these same traits are seen in Jesus' life. Joseph was a man of compassion - discuss specific examples where this trait is seen in Jesus' life. Joseph was a man who pondered over possible actions - discuss specific examples where this same trait is seen in Jesus' life. Joseph was a man who was obedient unto God - discuss specific examples where this same trait is seen in Jesus' life.

4. Search the Scriptures and discuss any other biblical dads that influenced their sons (or daughters) positively and/or negatively. Take time to pray that God would transform you, or a dad you know, to become more like the positive biblical role models of dads that you find.

5. Take time this week and ask your wife how she perceives you're doing as a dad. Ask her for positive ways you can improve. Take time this week and ask your children how they perceive you're doing as a dad. Ask them for positive ways you can improve. Cover the entire process with prayer that God would be glorified in the entire process from start to finish. If you are a wife, discuss the possibility of doing this with your husband and children. Discuss the possibility with friends who are dads.

Scripture

And there were shepherds living out in the fields nearby, keeping watch over their flocks at night. An angel of the Lord appeared to them, and the glory of the Lord shone around them, and they were terrified. But the angel said to them, "Do not be afraid. I bring you good news of great joy that will be for all people. Today in the town of David a Savior has been born to you, he is Christ the Lord. This will be a sign to you: you will find a baby wrapped in cloths and lying in a manger."

Suddenly a great company of heavenly host appeared with the angel, praising God and saying, "Glory to God in the highest, and on earth peace to men on whom his favor rests."

When the angels had left them and gone into heaven, the shepherds said to one another, "Let's go to Bethlehem and see this thing that has happened, which the Lord has told us about."

So they hurried off and found Mary and Joseph, and the baby, who was lying in the manger. When they had seen him, they spread the word concerning what had been told them about the child, and all who heard it were amazed at what the shepherds said to them. But Mary treasured up all these things and pondered them in her heart. The shepherds returned, glorifying and praising God for all they had heard and seen, which were just as they had been told (Luke 2:8–20).

Six

Fishing
with the
Angels

"Once upon a time . . ." "Peace on earth." "Goodwill among men." Sounds like the opening for a fairy tale.

Where is this peace of which the angels sang? Anger, bitterness, violence and hatred appear to permeate every corner of the United States. Scan page after page of virtually any newspaper in America. It's wearying to the soul.

"Man's inhumanity towards man" never ceases to sicken and sadden. "Peace among men"?

A glance at magazine headlines, like "America the Brutal," tells the story. The image of Rodney King being pummeled by police officers still haunts America's conscience. And what of Reginald Denny being pulled from his tractor-trailer rig and being bludgeoned by angry youth in Los Angeles as a result of the innocent verdict at King's trial?

Relations haven't visibly improved in the years since the above events occurred. Recently a man in Jasper, Texas was dragged behind a pickup truck for two miles down a dirt road. His crime? The color of his skin. His sentence? A brutal death.

The blood of students and teachers has intermingled at school yards and school halls over the last sixteen months.

Pearl, Miss: A sixteen-year-old kills his mother and then goes to school where he shoots nine students. Two of them die.

Paducah, Kentucky: A fourteen-year-old student kills three students and wounds five others while they are praying in a hallway at school. One of the wounded is left paralyzed.

Jonesboro, Arkansas: Two boys, ages eleven and thirteen, kill four girls and a teacher during a false alarm at school. Ten others are wounded.

And who will ever forget Columbine High School?

These high-profile reports are endemic of the millions of stories that daily go untold. Angry, abusive husbands lash out verbally and physically at their families; drivers with clenched fists are ready to do combat in the middle of the street over an errant lane change; youth draw guns to solve any number of problems; on and on the list could grow.

The negative effects of anger and hatred are reverberating across the entire global community. No place is safe from these negative repercussions, from the once pristine rural settings to the urban asphalt jungles. And the torrent appears to be ascending at an alarming rate as we approach the twenty-first century.

Was life really so different in the first century that the shepherds believed such a song? Were peace, goodwill, and harmony commonplace occurrences for these men?

No. Mankind has become more technologically advanced in the way he abuses and destroys. But hatred and violence seem to have been commonplace since Adam and Eve were kicked out of the Garden—remember Cain and Abel?

What were relations like in the shepherds' world when the angels sang their song? Well, the shepherds themselves were a despised group. They lived in temporary dwellings—they were not exactly upwardly mobile. The nature of their occupation oft-times made them "unclean" so they were unable to observe the Law's requirements. They couldn't follow the rules of ritual purity because of their jobs. Hence, if they were ceremonially unclean they couldn't participate in worship at the temple. Can you say, "outcasts"?

Say the word, "shepherd," and the first word that came to mind for many would be "thief." Shepherds also had no formal training in the study of the Law so they were considered ignorant.

They had three strikes against them: they were considered unclean, thieves, and ignorant. And these guys were exuberant at the angels' anthem?!!

Lest we think that these poor shepherds were the only one on the social hit list, don't forget the status of tax collectors, Samaritans, Scythian slaves, Gentiles, lepers . . .

Ever since the Israelites' return from Babylonian exile, foreign governments had placed heavy tax burdens upon them. For a fellow Jew to be in league with Israel's oppressors, as a tax collector, was detestable. Bitter hatred was exhibited towards such men. They were found so contemptible that they were placed completely outside of Jewish society. Can you say, "outcasts"?

Palestine at this time was divided into two main sections. Judea and Samaria were under the control of Roman procurators while Galilee and Perarea were under the power of Herod Antipas.

Ask a Jew about Samaria and they would scoff, or worse, at the idea of its being part of the Holy Land. The very term "Samaritan" was a slur Jews used to show reproach.

Consider the following insult hurled at Jesus: "The Jews answered him, 'Aren't we right in saying that you are a Samaritan and demon possessed?'" (John 8:48). The Samaritans were ranked with Gentiles and strangers. Can you say, "outcasts"?

And the list could grow. Gentiles, foreigners, lepers, at times women . . . Why were these shepherds so willing to believe the angels' song when they were daily enmeshed in such an oppressive social milieu?

Perhaps we need to back up to the beginning of the story, before the singing started, to find the hope that drove these shepherds forward.

1. "An angel of the Lord appeared to them"

Did you catch that? Who did the angel appear to—the rich, the famous, the governors, kings, the princes or the priests? No!

The angel appeared to the outcasts. Shepherds had one of the lowest occupations imaginable. People avoided them, and yet, the angel of the Lord came to them! What a joy for God's grace to come from the heavens upon this cluster of castaways.

> Remember, dear brothers and sisters, that few of you were wise in the world's eyes, or powerful, or wealthy when God called you. Instead, God deliberately chose things the world considers foolish in order to shame those who think they are wise. And he chose those who are powerless to shame those who are powerful. God chose things despised by the world, things counted as nothing at all, and used them to bring to nothing what the world considers important, so that no one can ever boast in the presence of God. (1 Corinthians 1:26–29, NLT)

Perhaps it shouldn't have been so surprising—remember the "man after God's own heart"? King David, the ancestor of the Anointed One, started his career as a "lowly shepherd boy." And remember that one of the Messiah's favorite monikers is "the Good Shepherd"?

> The spirit of the Sovereign Lord is upon me, because the Lord has appointed me to bring good news to the poor. He has sent me to comfort the brokenhearted and to announce that captives will be released and prisoners will be freed (Isaiah 61:1, NLT).

2. "...and the glory of the Lord shone around them"

These lowly shepherds witnessed the manifestation of God's presence, his Shekinah glory. If they had any inkling at all of their people's history, they would have known that this was the same glory that appeared to Abraham, that caused Moses' face to shine, that appeared in the tabernacle, that appeared in the temple, and that Ezekiel saw depart from the temple.

> Then the cherubim lifted their wings and rose into the air with their wheels beside them, and the glory of the God of Israel hovered above them. Then the glory of the Lord went up from the city and stopped above the mountain to the east (Ezekiel 11:22–23, NLT).

It had been over 400 years since Israel had seen a recorded, visible sign from God, a sign of His presence among His people. After this long absence, the glory of God is manifested before the shepherds in the field, not the priests in the temple.

3. "I bring you good news of great joy that will be for all people"

It just keeps getting better. Now the angel tells them that the good news of Israel's Savior being born includes them. It's "for all people"! The outcasts are included in the biggest party to come—the great banquet hall will have a place for them. The gates of heaven aren't slammed shut!

4. Then a multitude of angels sang, "Glory to God in the highest, and on earth peace among men on whom his favor rests"

Back to that song. I still don't see the peace and goodwill back then or now . . . Whoa! Wait a minute! Those poor ignorant shepherds understood the song more clearly and quickly than many of us who have sung the stanzas in centuries since.

The secret of "peace on earth and goodwill among men" was given on this night to the shepherds.

Do you see it?

We've been asking the wrong question! We need to start at the beginning of the song. Where is the "glory to God in the highest"?

We cannot expect man to be in right relationship with his fellow man unless he is first in a right relationship with God.

73

The secret of that peace and goodwill must first start with the individual's relationship with God. We will not see peace come to pass any other way.

It has not come through racial reconciliation groups.

It has not come through diversity training.

It has not come through sensitivity training.

It has not come through round-table discussions.

True, lasting "peace on earth, goodwill among men" will only come one way: Reconciliation with God (among whom God is well pleased), then reconciliation with man. This is the only path of peace available. All other efforts will mete out a seasonal cease-fire at best.

5. "Let's go to Bethlehem and see this thing that has happened, which the Lord told us about. So they hurried off..."

Is it any wonder?

The angel of the Lord appeared to them.

The glory of the Lord shone around them.

The good news included them.

The secret of peace was given to them.

They were not outcasts in the eyes of God. A chance to see God's son, Immanuel, the One who gave them hope, the Prince of Peace—"Let's Go!!!"

Nothing kept them from immediate action. What happened to their sheep? Who knows? Priorities! The Good Shepherd vs. the sheep.

6. "When they had seen him, they spread the word concerning what had been told them about the child..."

Who would have thought it? The shepherds became the first fishermen of the Christian era.

Salvation is offered to all people—including the poor, the outcasts, the have-nots. Peace is offered to all.

The impact of this good news upon their lives was such that they were compelled to go forward to "spread a passion for the supremacy of God [glory] in all things, for the joy of all peoples."[1]

7. "The shepherds returned, glorifying and praising God for all the things they had heard and seen, which were just as they had been told."

The final result was not a mountain top experience that faded quickly. The shepherds went back to their jobs, back to their daily routines, but they weren't the same.

Then, as now, coming fully into the presence of the Prince of Peace causes change. "The shepherds returned glorifying God."

They heard the angels' song. They understood the song. And now, they were living the song.

[1] Dr. John Piper, *A Godward Life* (Sisters, Oregon: Multnomah Publishers, 1997) 19.

Fishing Principle

*A right relationship with Jesus must come first!
When Christ's offer of a saving lordship for all
peoples, for His glory, is understood and accepted,
then we will understand the reason for fishing.
"And they lived happily ever after" will be a reality
someday for His followers. What a message to a
hurting world!*

STUDY QUESTIONS

1. Have you ever sung the famous stanza, "Peace on earth, goodwill toward men," and wondered if this has ever been true? Discuss why the shepherds were so willing to believe such a song when they, up to that point, had not experienced such peace and goodwill. Why should we believe such a song today? Have you ever had a glimpse of this peace and good-will in your life? Share how and when it happened. Could it be replicated?

2. Meditate and pray that the following verses would be-come a reality in your life — "and the glory of the Lord shone around them"; "I bring you good news of great joy that will be for all people." Pray also that you would be used of God as an instrument to make these verses a reality in the lives of others. Pray that you would be the Anointed One's ambassa-dor of peace and good will to your part of a broken and im-prisoned world. Ask the Holy Spirit to guide you to reach out to those He has prepared to hear the Good News of the An-gels in your neighborhood, workplace, congregation...

3. Read Luke 2:8-20 again and visualize that you are one of those shepherds. Imagine the bright light of God's glory! Imag-ine the angel speaking to you! Imagine a host of angels singing the Good News! Imagine hurrying off with your fellow shep-herds to see the Christ-child! Imagine the range of emotions pursing through your body as you look upon the Little One knowing He is the Hope of all Israel! Imagine the enthusiasm and discussions that occur as you head home! Visualize the same results occurring in your life as they did in the shepherds after they encountered Jesus — "The shepherds returned, glorifying and praising God for all they had heard and seen..."

4. Take time to praise Jesus that He came to earth to set prisoners free. Praise Him that He came to bring peace and good will to all people. Praise Him that your name is included on the list of people He came to bless. Praise Him that He sent His angels to sing of the glorious good news. Praise Him that His glory resides in you now because your body is the temple of the Holy Spirit. Praise Him because...

Scripture

The beginning of the gospel about Jesus Christ, the Son of God.

It is written in Isaiah the prophet:
"I will send my messenger ahead of you, who will prepare your way" —
"a voice of one calling in the desert, 'Prepare the way for the Lord, make straight paths for him.'"

And so John came, baptizing in the desert region and preaching a baptism of repentance for the forgiveness of sin. The whole Judean countryside and all the people of Jerusalem went out to him. Confessing their sins, they were baptized by him in the Jordan River. John wore clothing made of camel's hair, with a leather belt around his waist, and he ate locusts and wild honey. And this was his message: "After me will come one more powerful than I, the thongs of whose sandals I am not worthy to stoop down and untie. I baptize you with water, but he will baptize you with the Holy Spirit." (Mark 1:1-8)

Seven

Fishing
John *with* the Baptist

Mark Tuinei, Nate Newton, Ray Donaldson, Ron Stone, Larry Allen. Household names?

Maybe—if your television and your mind are preset for the football season. Or if you live in the Lone Star State, as I do. (But, shh, I'm still a Viking's fan from my college days.)

Back to those names. Who are these guys? These five men were the mainstay of the offensive line for the Dallas Cowboys' championship runs in the 1990s.

One of their jobs was to open up those gaping holes that announcers so blithely contend that, "even I could have run through a hole that big!" But that's another story.

If you desire accolades, do not become an offensive lineman. These are not the glory positions. "Men in the trenches" depicts the role they play.

Making clear paths though which the running backs could romp was a major part of their job description. In this case, their main mission was to protect Emmitt Smith, the man with the ball.

"Ah," you say, "now there's a name I recognize." He's one of those few that has arrived, by the world's standards.

No need to use two names. Just say "Emmitt" and people automatically picture that slashing style and smashing smile. The world's icons and heroes—Emmitt, Troy, Shaq, Hakeem, Deion.

Now, who did you say those offensive lineman were? Forgot already, didn't you?

These linemen knew that they were not going to receive the accolades, endorsements, or salaries of the marquee players. It goes with the position.

As disciples of Jesus, we must have a similar mindset. John the Baptizer (he wasn't really a Baptist, you know) understood this principle. His job was to prepare the way for the Messiah. He was not fishing for himself, but for the Ultimate Angler. John was casting the bait into the lake in preparation for the time when Jesus' reel would be whirling, hook arching through the air towards the water.

It didn't have to be this way. John could have just as easily positioned himself to be the marquee player in the eyes of the people. Here's a man whose birth was announced by an angel. Some considered him to be the first prophet sent to Israel in 400 years.

And, he definitely dressed the part—John wore clothing made of camel's hair, with a leather belt around his waist, and he ate locusts and wild honey. Clothing fit for a prophet.

His mindset was a radical departure from his fellow man's. Jesus testified to this very fact: "Who is this man in the wilderness that you went out to see? Did you find him weak as a reed, moved by every breath of wind? Or were you expecting to see a man dressed in expensive clothes? Those who dress like that live in palaces, not out in the wilderness" (Matthew 11:7–8, NLT).

John's very lifestyle seemed to be a living sermon against all self-indulgence and selfishness. Calling John an ascetic would be an understatement. He did not wear the latest fashions, unless *Prophecy Wear* was a designer label. He also didn't seek the finest in food on which to indulge himself. I doubt locusts and wild honey were being served at *Chez Jerusalem.*

People were curious—was John the Messiah, the one they had been so desperately waiting for? "The people were waiting expectantly and were all wondering in their hearts if John might possibly be the Christ" (Luke 3:15). All John had to do was answer one question affirmatively and he would have been number one in many people's eyes. He had an opening, a straight shot to the top.

In fact, John's popularity was so great that some Jewish and Gentile leaders alike feared his influence. Josephus, the Jewish historian, recorded in his *Antiquities* that Herod was so afraid of John's following that he feared it might lead to rebellion against the government. Even after John's death, some Jewish leaders still feared the lingering effects of John's popularity (cf. Mark 11:27–33).

What was John's response to this attention?

> Now this was John's testimony when the Jews of Jerusalem sent priests and Levites to ask him who he was. He did not fail to confess, but confessed freely, "I am not the Christ . . . I am the voice of one calling in the desert, 'Make straight the way for the Lord'" (John 1:19–20, 23).

The entire focus of John the Baptizer's life was on the coming Messiah. As evidenced by his message and lifestyle, he was not intent on bringing glory and accolades to himself. John wanted people to know that they had to be willing to give up the stuff of life to which they so desperately clung. He showed people how little they truly needed to live. By baptizing and preaching in the wilderness, John caused people to leave their daily luxuries, for a while at least, and focus on the essentials of life.

John did not serve two masters and he allowed the children of Israel to see a sermon rather than merely hear one. And what was the sermon title they saw? "He must become greater; I must become less. The one who comes from above is above all" (John 3:30–31a).

81

This message is the opposite of the media slogans that constantly bombard us, and that we often buy into: *McDonald's* espouses, "You deserve a break today," while *Burger King* advises, "Have it your way." Newer, bigger, brighter, bolder. The skewed goal of merely keeping up with the Jones' is not even good enough today. Too many of us desire to *be* the mythical Jones family while *MasterCard* massages our consumerist mentality with: *"MasterCard,* so worldly, so welcome."

It's not quite the same bait that John used to draw people in.

Did he promise, "Have it your way"? Did he use a catchy jingle? The latest church growth techniques? Direct mail or television advertising blitzes? Previous successful crusades? Massive stadiums with elaborate sound systems and direct-link hook-ups? (I'm still not sure what these are, but they seem to be a must for the big fishing trips). There is nothing wrong with some of these methods, but the average disciple can feel unqualified to go fishing without them.

John's message was one of repentance—supposedly not a big drawing card, then or now. He was calling the Jewish people to have a radical change of mind and heart, leave their sins, and turn to God for forgiveness. This was no little matter. John was calling the children of Abraham to repentance, baptism, and confession of their sins.

Consider the fact that the only time someone was baptized through immersion in a once-for-all-time manner was when non-Jews converted to Judaism (proselyte baptism). The Jewish mindset believed that the end-all, be-all of repenting was when a non-Jew was baptized. Now, suddenly, John was asking Jews to do the same thing required of the Gentiles!!!

In essence, John was letting them know that simply being a Jew was not enough to assure them a place in God's kingdom. Their sins made them the same as the Gentiles—they needed the same radical surgery to remove the cancerous growth. John warned, "And do not think you can say to yourselves, 'We have Abraham as our father.' I tell you that out of these stones God can raise up children for Abraham" (Matthew 3:9, Luke 3:8).

John dared to preach an offensive message in order to help save his people. He feared not the human backlash against him, but rather the backlash that would occur on judgment day if the nation of Israel did not respond positively to God's message. It was a message spoken out of love for God and for His people.

Not only was John's message tough to swallow but his wilderness location seemed hardly ideal for attracting crowds. God, however, seemed to choose this desolate region in order to draw people away from their normal patterns, professions, and pleasures. Perhaps it was to remind them of the desert wanderings Israel endured for forty years. It was time to reflect on their failure to enter the promised land, a time to extend God's grace to His people AGAIN!

It is estimated that Jerusalem is at least 20 miles from where John could have baptized at the Jordan River. Couple this with a 4,000 foot elevation drop down to the Jordan. Who would want to travel that distance to a desolate region with the knowledge they had to travel the same distance back up—4,000 feet?

What was the result? "The entire Judean countryside and all of Jerusalem came out to him"! Amazing. This is clearly an exaggeration, but it does not minimize the huge numbers that flocked to see John in action. Scholars estimate that somewhere between 200,000 to 500,000 people were baptized by John in approximately a year's span!

Now that's some fishing trip.

His success rested on the fact that he understood his role. John knew he was the forerunner, the messenger. He did not even consider himself worthy to stoop down and untie the sandals of the Messiah. And this was his message: "After me will come one more powerful than I, the thongs of whose sandals I am not worthy to stoop down and untie" (Mark 1:2). Jewish tradition taught that the difference between a disciple and a servant was that a disciple would do every service requested by his master that the lowest servant would do—except the untying of the master's sandals in order that they could be cleaned. Yet, John did not even consider himself worthy to do this most menial task for the Messiah. John knew his position and relished it. He was truly a humble man.

Can we say the same? Are we content to simply prepare the way? As disciples of Jesus we must prepare the way for Him to be introduced into people's lives. That is our role. We, like John, are not in the glory positions. Accolades are not for us. Glory belongs unto God alone:

> Therefore God exalted him to the highest place and gave him the name that is above every name, that at the name of Jesus every knee should bow, in heaven and on earth and under the earth, and every tongue confess that Jesus Christ is Lord, to the glory of God the Father" (Philippians 2:9–11).

Fishing Principle

Fish with Humility. Turn the spotlight on the Giver of every good and perfect gift. Do not seek to have your name recognized. Seek to magnify the Name that is above every other name—Jesus, just one Name!

STUDY QUESTIONS

1. Have you ever been involved in a ministry in your local congregation and were not recognized as being a participant? Discuss how that made you feel. If you felt neglected, what were you expecting to receive from your role in the ministry? Are you content in simply preparing the way? Take time to sing the song, "Jesus, Name above All Names."

2. Read and meditate upon Galatians 2:20, Philippians 2:9-11, and John 3:30-31. Take time to pray and ask the Holy Spirit that these verses would become a moment-by-moment reality in your life.

3. What do you think of John's radical departure in lifestyle from his fellow man? Why do you think he dressed and ate so peculiarly? Can you think of any modern-day Christian leaders doing similar things? How do their lifestyle and message, or John's, make you feel when you examine your life? Take time to pray that the Holy Spirit would help you to have a discerning heart to recognize the great chasm that lies between needs and wants; and between entertaining and illuminating - and to choose wisely!

4. Is John's message being boldly proclaimed or is it a faint echo at best? Take time to pray that the reality of Romans 3:23 and the glorious grace of Romans 6:23 would be preached and taught in your home and congregation. Pray for your pastor(s) to have bold preaching that does not fear if the Gospel offends but rather fears what will occur on Judgment Day for those left unredeemed. Pray for the Holy Spirit to open blind eyes and hardened hearts that many will come to be baptized in the name of the Father, the Son, and the Holy Spirit.

5. Read and meditate upon Acts 2. Visualize yourself as Peter, as another disciple, as an unbelieving Jew. See and feel the Holy Spirit come mightily upon you. Hear the disciples speak in a myriad of tongues. Be amazed at Peter's bold preaching. Praise God for those who were "cut to the heart" and asked, "Brothers what shall we do?" Take time to pray for a

fresh outpouring of the Holy Spirit upon you and your congregation that great numbers would be added to the Lamb's
Book of Life.

Scripture

At that time Jesus came from Nazareth in Galilee and was baptized by John in the Jordan. As Jesus was coming up out of the water, he saw heaven being torn open and the Spirit descending on him like a dove. And a voice came from heaven: "You are my Son, whom I love; with you I am well pleased."

At once the Spirit sent him out into the desert, and he was in the desert forty days, being tempted by Satan. He was with the wild animals, and angels attended him. (Mark 1:9–13)

Eight

Fishing
Holy Spirit
with the

"It's time."

Normally the trip from Spearman to Amarillo, 100 miles, is a relatively uneventful drive. But Wednesday, August 28, 1991, was not to be a typical day.

At 4:00 in the afternoon Lea began having what she believed were mild contractions. "Today is the day our baby is going to be born," she announced.

After ten months of pregnancy and numerous stories of Braxton-Hicks contractions (false alarms) from well-meaning mothers, I politely answered, "That would be fine with me, Dear."

I might be a slow learner, but there was one thing I had learned by this point in time. Agreeing with a pregnant woman is the best way to avoid "the look." However, I wasn't really expecting the miraculous event to be as foretold by my wife. After all, we had just been to the doctor the previous day and she wasn't dilated at all.

At 8:00 that evening while singing in church, Lea nudged me in the ribs whenever a contraction hit: "Eight minutes apart, ouch; four minutes, ouch; seven minutes, ouch; three minutes, ouch; eight minutes, ouch!" They don't tell you about this kind of variation between contractions (or the subsequent pain in the ribs) in any classes we took!

Cool, calm, and collected—NOT. At 8:30, I convinced Lea that we should call the doctor because I was getting concerned—okay, worried! First child.

The doctor called back at 8:45 (that's right, we had to talk to the answering service and convince them it was important enough to interrupt him). The doctor told Lea that we could come to the hospital. But, he'd just end up sending us home because she wouldn't be dilated enough. After all, he reminded us, she wasn't dilated at all just the day before.

Okay, just relax and keep timing those contractions. No sense making that long drive just to turn around and come right back home. The doctor's the expert. He's been through hundreds of these events. Besides, they said we would have plenty of time to make it to the hospital when her contractions were between five and seven minutes apart. And surely that won't happen tonight.

"Four minutes, four minutes, four minutes...," a mere forty minutes after talking to the doctor.

I wasn't expecting the contractions to start going backwards to get us back up between five and seven minutes—when I'd have plenty of time to get Lea to the hospital.

PANIC. Suddenly all those shows about the goofy, stumbling, bumbling, father-to-be seemed all too realistic. "We need to call the doctor back NOW." Another phone call, another lovely chat with the answering service.

We waited patiently for the call back (HAH!). "Come on down. I'll tell the hospital you'll be there in about two hours. Don't be surprised if we just end up sending you back home."

He didn't seem too concerned (or alarmed) about Lea's progress. For me, however, the same could not be said. Lea has a high threshold of pain and she was doing more than just wincing.

For every day of Lea's pregnancy we had prayed for plenty of time to get to the hospital, and that once we got there, it would be a relatively short amount of time before the baby was born. No marathon birthing sessions was the prayer of the season.

We'd had the Bronco packed for days (the vehicle, not the horse—we had no desire to emulate Mary and Joseph's donkey travels). Talk about a road trip to the hospital. I wonder what Joseph was thinking? Did the angel tell him he'd have plenty of time to make it to Bethlehem? "Don't worry Joseph. A room will be waiting for you."

In contrast to the pre-birth travels of the Messiah, we simply had to get in our vehicle and drive. The doctor's words echoed in my ears, "No problem, plenty of time." Yet, somehow they were not very reassuring.

Sweaty palmed and cotton-mouthed, 70 m.p.h was our beginning speed. After all, the doctor figured we had plenty of time. Thirty miles outside of Amarillo that little Bronco's speedometer was pegged and we had no idea how fast we were traveling. Not fast enough for Lea!

Lea was in tremendous pain and the contractions were two minutes or less apart. We were progressing just a little faster than the doctor anticipated (Lea's contractions and my driving). We travelled so fast through Amarillo that it looked like one of those small-dots-on-a-map-if-you-blink-you-miss-it towns.

"The time has come." At 11:20 p.m we landed at the hospital emergency exit. While prepping for Lea's initial exam, the labor/delivery nurse asked Lea if her doctor had discussed the possibility of using any medication to help ease the pain.

"I want some!" Lea grimaced.

"Oh, sorry. Too late," the nurse exuded. "You're fully dilated. Get ready to have a baby."

"But, that's not possible," I silently fumed. "This is not how the doctor said it would be."

No private, cushy, birthing suite for us. At 11:50 p.m. we were rushed into a delivery room because the doctor had not arrived. It was a cold, sterile, metallic setting resonating with a sense of emergency. No doctor, but a team of neonatal nurses, ...just in case.

It was 12:00 midnight, still no doctor. He didn't believe the time was right. He wasn't prepared. The expert was about to meet the true Keeper of Time.

At 12:03 the doctor finally arrived. At 12:07 Madeline Alexis Schrader made her triumphant entry into this world. Baffled by the timing of this miraculous event, all the doctor could do was shake his head and mumble a pseudo-apology: "It shouldn't have been time."

Timing. It's essential for every good fisherman and fisherwoman. At high noon on a summer day you might catch a good tan out on the lake, but not many, if any, fish.

Why? Timing. Too hot and the fish are submerged towards the bottom of the lake. Out the line goes time and time again with nary a bite. Finally the worms are all drowned and you decide to call it a day.

"What happened?" you ask yourself. "I used the best worms and the fish still didn't come."

There's a lot more to fishing than simply providing "good bait." You also need to find out what the best time is to cast out your line and the best time to call it a day, to "fish or cut bait."

Jesus knew where and when the fish would be biting and when it was time to "cut bait." Consider the following interchange between the Lord and Simon Peter:

> When he had finished speaking, he said to Simon, "Put out into deep water, and let down the nets for a catch." Simon answered, "Master, we've worked hard all night and haven't caught anything. But because you say so, I will let down the nets." When they had done so, they caught such a large number of fish that their nets began to break. So they signaled their partners in the other boat to come and help them, and they came and filled both boats so full that they began to sink (Luke 5:5–7).

Every fisherman's dream (or tale)!

Why were Simon and his companions so successful? They had a Guide showing them when and where to let out their nets. They followed His instructions, even though they seemed somewhat absurd at the time.

You can almost sense it in Simon's response, "Master, we've worked hard all night and haven't caught anything." It's as if Simon was attempting to remind Jesus that the best time to fish is at night—and that had been a bust. They had an empty boat to prove it. Yet, Simon and his companions hesitatingly followed the Lord's leading: "But because you say so, I will let down the nets."

"And the rest," as they say, "is history."

Unfortunately, however, there were also times that Jesus had to "cut bait" because the fishing was sparse at best:

> Jesus said to them, "Only in his home town, among his relatives and in his own house is a prophet without honor." He could not do any miracles there, except lay his hands on a few sick people and heal them. And he was amazed at their lack of faith (Mark 6:4–5).

How was Jesus able to discern when to fish and when to move on? In order to fulfill His Father's will, and be the Fisherman of fishermen, Jesus' humanity needed the empowering of the Holy Spirit.

Acts 10:37–38 states,

> "You know what has happened throughout Judea, beginning in Galilee after the baptism that John preached—how God anointed Jesus of Nazareth with the Holy Spirit and power, and how he went around doing good and healing all who were under the power of the devil, because God was with him."

I know it is a mystery how it all works, but Jesus was fully God and fully man. His human side apparently needed the anointing and empowering of the Holy Spirit before His ministry began. His humanity needed the Holy Spirit for a successful catch or release program—"Fish or cut bait."

"That's great," you say, "but Jesus was/is God. He had a distinct advantage over us." Really? Remember, Acts 10:38? "God anointed Jesus of Nazareth with the Holy Spirit and power, and he went around doing good and healing all who were under the power of the devil, because God was with him."

Are we not anointed with that same Holy Spirit? Are our bodies not the temples of the Holy Spirit? "Do you not know that your body is a temple of the Holy Spirit, who is in you, whom you have received from God?" (1 Corinthians 6:19). The Holy Spirit takes up residence in the body of every believer.

The critical condition that needs to be met in fishing is not merely what bait you use—how many books on evangelism you have or haven't read. Nor is it your past experience or lack thereof; number of evangelism seminars attended; not even how many Billy Graham Evangelistic Crusades you have personally attended, or taped and memorized. Don't get me wrong, these can all be worthy facets of evangelism—but they're not the foundation on which it stands.

We need to have a Guide or a Fish Finder—someone who senses the movement in the water and lets you know, "This is the spot to drop your line." The place where the fish are swarming and searching for food. Or conversely, "Time to pack it up and move on."

If Jesus' humanity apparently needed the Holy Spirit as a Fish Finder, doesn't it make sense that we need to tap into that same source?

"Great," you say. "But I haven't heard an audible voice from God lately. Nor have I felt the Holy Spirit, like some Christians attest, driving me towards someone or somewhere. How am I supposed to know what the Holy Spirit wants me to do?"

The Holy Spirit wants us to fish. On that we must first agree. We are called to fish for men:

> Jesus came and told his disciples, "I have been given complete authority in heaven and on earth. Therefore, go, and make disciples of all the nations [fishing], bap-

tizing them in the name of the Father and the Son and the Holy Spirit. Teach these new disciples to obey all the commands I have given you. And be sure of this: I am with you always, even to the end of the age." (Matthew 28:18–20, NLT)

But when the Holy Spirit has come upon you, you will receive power and will tell people about me everywhere—in Jerusalem, throughout Judea, in Samaria, and to the ends of the earth (Acts 1:8, NLT).

"Agreed," you say, "we are commanded to fish. But the question still remains, where does God want me to fish, and who am I fishing for? How am I supposed to tap into that promised power?"

Perhaps we need to look at how Jesus made sure that He was on the right fishing trip. Where did He get His power from?

We read that immediately after Jesus was baptized, He was tempted by Satan in the desert. The temptation was for Jesus to abandon His fishing trip, to take a different, easier path, to cut bait (cf, Matthew 4:3–11, Luke 4:3–13). How did Jesus stay on the right path? How did He know which way to go to the proper fishing hole? How did He know it wasn't time to "cut bait" and scratch the whole fishing expedition?

With every attempt Satan made to thwart the fishing trip, Jesus responded with verbatim quotations from the Word of God—"It is written...", "It is written...", "It is written..."

Jesus knew which path to traverse because He used the Sword of the Spirit:

Take the helmet of salvation and the sword of the Spirit, which is the word of God [the Bible]. And pray in the Spirit, on all occasions with all kinds of prayers and requests. With this in mind, be alert and always keep on praying for all the saints (Ephesians 6:18–19).

Jesus was filled with the Spirit through baptism and equipped by the Spirit through study of God's Word.

How many times have we started a day and put stock in our own abilities as fishermen or fisherwomen? How many days have we headed out the door, pole in hand, enthusiasm gushing to overflow? How many times have we gone fishing without consulting our Fish Finder?

We must stay alert. We must use God's Word as our primary guide—to remind us that we are called to fish, and to learn how to reel 'em in. We must study the timeless principles practiced by Jesus and His disciples.

We must take time to listen to where and how we are told to fish, even if it doesn't make sense at first. Look at what happened when Simon Peter listened.

Wouldn't it be something to see a boat so full of fish that it begins to sink?

Fishing Principle

*Seek the Holy Spirit's guidance through prayer
and study of the Word. A sword in its sheath is a
worthless weapon. Sensitivity to the Spirit will
help you know when to fish and when to
"cut bait."*

STUDY QUESTIONS

1. How do you know when it's time to share the gospel with someone - when it's time to go fishing? Is there such a thing as a window of opportunity? Is there such a thing as the right time, or is it anytime, anywhere, anyone? When did you seek to become a disciple of Jesus? Why at that moment in your life? Why not years earlier or years later? What do you think caused you to be receptive to the gospel at that moment in time?

2. Read the introduction to this book again (or for the first time). Why do you think these young men were so apprehensive about sharing the gospel? They had been "trained" and fish abounded, so what was the problem? Have you ever had an experience like this in your life? Discuss "mastering a method" versus listening to the "Master of methods." Take time to meditate on 1 Corinthians 3:5-7 and pray that you understand your role versus God's role in fishing expeditions. Put your name in place of Paul's and Apollos' as you meditate on the passage.

3. Discuss how the Holy Spirit guides us in our day-to-day lives through Scripture, through events in our lives, through the body of Christ, through that still small voice - the stirrings of the Spirit. Discuss specific examples from your own life how the Holy Spirit guided you through one of these means.

4. Read and discuss Acts 8:26-40. Visualize yourself in Philip's place. What would have been going through your mind? Take time to pray that you would have the same sensitivity and openness to the Spirit's guidance when He calls you to fish. We must look beyond the physical into the spiritual world!

5. Read and discuss Luke 5:5-7. How do you think Jesus was using this to prepare Peter, and others, to become "fishers of men?" Have you ever had an experience where the Holy Spirit guided you to fish for an individual, group, or family? Discuss what transpired from call to action. Read and discuss

Acts 10. Why was Peter so successful in fishing for Cornelius and his family? Take time to pray for the Holy Spirit to move like this in your life so the Cornelius' of today may come to know Jesus as Lord and Savior!

Scripture

The next day John was there again with two of his disciples. When he saw Jesus passing by, he said, "Look, the Lamb of God!"

When the two disciples heard him say this, they followed Jesus. Turning around, Jesus saw them following and asked, "What do you want?"

They said, "Rabbi" (which means Teacher), "where are you staying?"

"Come," he replied, "and you will see."

So they went and saw where he was staying and spent that day with him. It was about the tenth hour.

Andrew, Simon Peter's brother, was one of the two who heard what John had said and who had followed Jesus. The first thing Andrew did was to find his brother Simon and tell him, "We have found the Messiah" (that is, the Christ). And he brought him to Jesus.

Jesus looked at him and said, "You are Simon son of John. You will be called Cephas" (which, when translated, is Peter) (John 1:35–42).

Nine

Fishing
with
Andrew

She said, "Yes!"

The moment Lea said she would marry me transformed who I was, and who I was to become. Life would never be the same again. Two would become one!

We sat side-by-side with what seemed like permanent smiles on our faces and hearts. Number after number was dialed as we joyfully shared the news. We wasted no time informing our family and friends.

Becoming a disciple of Christ should be much the same. We need to realize that we have THE Good News—the Gospel (evangelion). The excitement that Lea and I had about sharing our engagement news should pale in comparison with wanting to share THE Good News first with our family and friends.

Often times, however, our enthusiasm and desire are not apparent because our focus has drifted. We forget where we were before the Lord entered our lives and changed us forever. We become mired in the humdrum of daily living and forget the masses who are still shackled by Satan and sin.

THE Good News should create in us, as disciples, a passionate desire for the unsaved to see and hear of our Lord Jesus Christ.

Have the mundane movements of daily life blotted out memories of the utter joy when you first received Jesus as your Lord and Savior? Perhaps meditating upon one of the Gospel narratives will bring you back to your First Love, and cause you to, "Go, therefore, and make disciples of all the nations... (Matthew 28:19).

Think back to when you graduated from high school or college. Did you keep that news to yourself? When you got that job promotion that you worked so hard for, did you keep silent? If God has blessed you with a spouse, what did you do when you became engaged? Any children? Bet you didn't waste any time letting your family and friends know about those bundles of blessings!

We naturally desire to share the good news that impacts our lives. So it was with Andrew when he met the Messiah!

And it all began when John the Baptizer shared THE Good News that he had been made privy to by the Holy Spirit. John was walking along with two of his disciples when he pointed to Jesus and said, "Look, the Lamb of God!" John stayed true to his calling, his humility, and released his disciples so they could go after, "He that is greater."

Andrew and the other disciple of the Baptizer didn't hesitate to follow after Jesus. After all, they had heard John speak of, "the Lamb of God that takes away the sins of the world." If this man was truly the Savior, they would be fools not to follow him.

The domino effect had begun.

When Jesus saw them following, He posed that familiar question, "What do you want?" He never forces Himself upon anyone. He is continually asking, "What can I do for you?" and waiting for a reply.

At first glance, Andrew's answer seems a bit strange: "Rabbi, where are you staying?" This is not the first question that wells up from my soul when I put myself in Andrew's shoes before the potential Savior of the world! But Andrew and the other disciple understood the ancient Semitic world much better than I. First, by addressing Jesus as "Rabbi" they were intimating that they wanted to be His disciples. It was the customary form of address towards one's teacher. One word, "Rabbi," let Jesus know that these men desired to learn the Truth—to become disciples of the Master.

Secondly, these two men weren't merely making small talk by asking, "Where are you staying?" They weren't concerned with his mailing address or the social status that Jesus' home might allot Him according to the standards of the day. These two men weren't satisfied in making a commitment to this Messiah based solely upon the hearsay evidence of the Baptizer. They wanted a firsthand experience with Jesus—a chance to find out if this truly was the "Lamb of God" John had preached about.

Andrew and his cohort were letting Jesus know that a passing glance, a cursory conversation, a chance meeting along the way wouldn't satisfy their thirst. A few minutes wasn't enough to answer their questions. They desired to fellowship with Jesus. Oh, to sit at the feet of the one they hoped was the Master!

Nothing else seemed to matter. For it was about the tenth hour (4:00 p.m.) when this request was made. Only two hours of sunlight would be left before they would have to search for a place to spend the night. But this, apparently, was not even an issue. Oh, to sit at the feet of the one they hoped was the Master!

There were no other priorities, a lesson to be learned for us all—"Christianity is not a convenience."

What was Jesus' response to this first step towards Him?

"Come and see." Jesus doesn't hesitate a moment. He extends an invitation to these two men to come and see where he lives. Jesus sees a teachable moment and latches onto it immediately. There is no waiting until another time.

Jesus puts Himself at our disposal because our salvation will lead to the Father's glorification, which is the ultimate priority. When an unsaved individual truly desires to know more about the Risen Lord, His answer is the same yesterday, today, and forever: "Come and see...."

> "Here I am! I stand at the door and knock. If anyone hears my voice and opens the door, I will come in and eat with him, and he with me" (Revelation 3:20).

The result? Andrew and his friend become the first disciples of Jesus. And, "the first thing Andrew did was to find his brother Simon and tell him, 'We have found the Messiah.'"

So you don't have a seminary education. You're not an eloquent speaker or a leader in the church...so what? Did Andrew wait until he had it all together before he told a member of his family THE Good News? No! His encounter with the Messiah convinced him that Jesus was the Real Thing. He wasted no time searching for his brother so that Simon might meet the Messiah, too.

It's one thing to call Jesus the Messiah, or Lord and Savior as followers of Jesus do today. It's quite another thing to show a true conviction to those titles with action—by fishing.

Are the fish in your family waiting to bite? Andrew wasn't certain what Simon's response would be either. However, Andrew had "tasted of the Lord and saw that He was good" (Psalm 34:8). Andrew wanted to offer Simon that same chance.

> "Come, let us go up to the mountain of the Lord, to the house of the God of Jacob. He will teach us his ways, so that we may walk in his paths" (Isaiah 2:3).

Notice, Andrew didn't sit his brother down and instruct him in Theology 101. He simply said, "We have found the Messiah," and "then he brought Simon to Jesus." Andrew provided the introduction, Jesus provided the instruction.

Sometimes a simple introduction is the best bait. Perhaps the instruction will be left to another member of the body. This seems to be Andrew's modus operandi. He is not a well-known individual outside of the lists of the apostles. Yet, the three times we do meet him he is introducing someone to Jesus.

First, he introduces his brother to Jesus. The result? Jesus fishes for Peter by showing him his potential: "You are Simon son of John. You will be called Cephas" (which, when translated, is Peter). In the Greek, Peter is *petros* and rock is *petra.*

A person's name in the ancient world meant much more than it does to most of us today. It wasn't merely a label so people could differentiate one person from another. For a person such as Peter, a name was a reflection of one's true personality, a summation of the whole person in one word!

But a person does not need to remain what he has been, nor is his nature forever determined by the name first given to him. This can be seen in several Old Testament references to a change in one's name, and with it a concomitant change in character and conduct. The new name signifies a new beginning, a new opportunity, a new position, a new person.[1]

This is exactly what Jesus does. He gives Simon a new name to let him know what he could and would become in Him, "The Rock." None need stay the same. An introduction to Jesus can transform a life for eternity—"a new beginning, a new opportunity, a new position, a new person."

Hope springs eternal.

Even a cursory glance at the life of Peter in the Gospels shows him to be anything but "The Rock." He is the one who acts upon impulse. He is the one who flies off the handle at times. He is the one who can't be counted on—"I tell you the truth," Jesus answered, "this very night, before the rooster crows, you will disown me three times" (Matthew 26:34).

And yet, Jesus knew this would not be the last word spoken regarding Peter. This was still the man of whom the Lord said, "And I tell you that you are Peter, and on this rock I will build my church, and the gates of Hades will not overcome it" (Matthew 16:18).

---

[1] F.G. Hawhorne, *International Standard Bible Encyclopedia,* vol.3 (Grand Rapids, Michigan: William B. Eardmans Publishing Co., G.W. Bromiley, Gen. Ed., 1986) Names, 482.

Jesus showed Peter the possibilities—what he would become. A study of the Book of Acts shows that Peter did, in fact, become The Rock of the early church. The man who once fled from the mere perception of a relationship with Christ stood up in Jerusalem on the day of Pentecost and preached boldly of his Lord and Savior: "Those who accepted his message were baptized, and about three thousand were added to their number that day" (Acts 2:41). John the Baptizer points two disciples towards Jesus. Andrew introduces his brother Simon to Jesus, and he becomes the first-fruits of Jesus' disciples. Quite a beginning!

Can you imagine what the early church might have been like if Andrew hadn't made that introduction?

But Andrew didn't stop there. Secondly, we see him behind the scenes at the feeding of the five thousand. "Another of his disciples, Andrew, Simon Peter's brother, spoke up, 'Here is a boy with five small barley loaves and two small fish, but how far will they go among so many?'" (John 6:8–9). How far indeed!

And it all started when Andrew introduced a boy to the Anointed One.

Lastly, we see Andrew even introducing some Gentiles to Jesus. "Now there were some Greeks among those who went up to worship at the Feast. They came to Philip who was from Bethsaida in Galilee, with a request. 'Sir,' they said, 'we would like to see Jesus.' Philip went to tell Andrew; Andrew and Philip in turn told Jesus" (John 12:20–22).

Is there someone you need to simply introduce to Jesus in order for a life to be forever changed? Or perhaps there is someone in your life, like Simon, who needs to know what his or her potential is in the Lord, what he or she can become.

Remember, use different bait for different fish. Two brothers grew up with the same parents, in the same home, in the same synagogue, in the same city. And yet, Jesus didn't fish for them in the same way. Andrew needed more instruction and time with the Lord. Simon needed a new identity.

Jesus' fishing methods while He walked the earth changed to meet the needs of each individual. So must ours. "He who has ears, let him hear" (Matthew 13:9).

Fishing Principle

*1. Point people towards the Way of forgiveness.
John the Baptizer said, "Behold the Lamb of God
who takes away the sins of the world."
2. Give a priority to relationships, not schedules.
Jesus said, "Come and see."
3. Introduce family and friends to the Lord. "The
first thing Andrew did was to find his brother...."
4. Show people the possibilities of one whose life is
surrendered to Jesus. "...you will be called Peter."
5. Someone has to fish in foreign waters like
Andrew did with the Greeks (see Acts 1:8).*

STUDY QUESTIONS

1. What is the greatest event that has taken place in your life that you couldn't wait to tell all your family and friends? Have you ever had that same excitement in sharing the Gospel with anyone? Discuss your experience. Why do you believe the excitement, drive, passion in sharing the Gospel is not readily apparent in many of our lives? Take time to pray for the Holy Spirit to build a passion, desire, enthusiasm for your family and friends to come to a saving relationship with Jesus. Pray that you might be the vessel through which they see and hear the Good News.

2. Visualize yourself in Andrew's place as you read John 1:35-42. Discuss: What feelings would you experience as John the Baptist pointed to the "Lamb of God"? What would go through your mind as you and the "other disciple" followed behind Jesus? What would you say when Jesus turned around and asked, "What do you want?" What would you do after spending private time at the feet of Jesus?

3. What did Andrew do after spending time alone with Jesus? Why do you think he did this? Are there any fish in your family that might be waiting to "bite"? Take time to pray for those family members that they will experience Psalm 34:8 in their lives. Ask the Holy Spirit to provide an opportunity for you to introduce your family members to Jesus. Believe that Isaiah 2:3 will be a reality in the relationship - that God will provide the necessary instruction once you provide the introduction.

4. Is there someone you need to simply introduce to Jesus in order for his/her life to be forever changed? Or is there someone in your life, like Simon, who needs to know what his/her potential is in the Lord, what he/she can become?

5. Take time to pray and ask the Holy Spirit to reveal to you the special qualities He sees in the family member(s) you are fishing for. Ask the Holy Spirit to help you to be sensitive to teachable moments where you can encourage your family member(s) by revealing those qualities/potentials the Lord sees in them.

Scripture

While he {Jesus} was by the lake, one of the synagogue rulers, named Jairus, came there. Seeing Jesus, he fell at his feet and pleaded earnestly with him, "My little daughter is dying. Please come and put your hands on her so that she will be healed and live." So Jesus went with him.

While Jesus was still speaking, some men came from the house of Jairus, the synagogue ruler. "Your daughter is dead," they said. "Why bother the teacher any more?"

Ignoring what they said, Jesus told the synagogue ruler, "Don't be afraid; just believe."

He did not let anyone follow him except Peter, James and John the brother of James. When they came to the home of the synagogue ruler, Jesus saw a commotion with people crying and wailing loudly. He went in and said to them, "Why all this commotion and wailing? The child is not dead but asleep." But they laughed at him.

After he put them all out, he took the child's father and mother and the disciples who were with him, and went in where the child was. He took her by the hand and said to her, "Talith Koum!" (which means, "Little girl, I say to you, get up!"). Immediately the girl stood up and walked around (she was twelve years old). At this they were completely astonished. He gave strict orders not to let anyone know about this, and told them to give her something to eat.
(Mark 5:21c–24; 35–43)

Ten

Fishing
Children *with*

Since before the Exodus from Egypt, God has received the full attention of parents through their children. Many other means may fail to get through to parents, but issues dealing with the welfare of their children tend to make them sit bolt upright and listen.

Consider the initial response from the Israelites when Moses tells them that God is going to set them free from the bondage of Pharoah:

> Then the Lord said to Moses, "Now you will see what I will do to Pharaoh: Because of my mighty hand he will let them go; because of my mighty hand he will drive them out of his country."
>
> Therefore, say to the Israelites, "I am the Lord, and I will bring you out from under the yoke of the Egyptians. I will free you from being slaves to them, and I will redeem you with an outstretched arm and with mighty acts of judgment. I will take you as my own people, and I will be your God. Then you will know that I am the Lord your God, who brought you out from

under the yoke of the Egyptians. And I will bring you to the land I swore with uplifted hand to give to Abraham, to Isaac and to Jacob. I will give it to you as a possession. I am the Lord."

Moses reported this to the Israelites, but they did not listen to him because of their discouragement and cruel bondage (Exodus 6:1, 6–9).

God promises to free the Israelites, His people, from beneath the crushing weight of Egyptian oppression and what is their response? "They did not listen"!

WOW! You would have thought Moses would have commanded the Israelites' full attention with his message from the Almighty. Freedom and redemption from slavery apparently weren't enough.

Do you think some of the people's minds were changed as the events of the following days unfolded? What happens in the minds of the masses as the plagues descend upon Egypt one-by-one? Imagine lying side-by-side with your spouse staring up at the starry sky from your dwelling place in Goshen.

"Maybe Moses was right, dear. After all, we have never seen anything like this happen before."

"I know, I know. First all the water in the land turned to blood. Blood in the buckets, blood in the jars. Blood, blood, blood. The Nile flowed crimson red and the stench from all the dead fish was unbearable!"

"And then the deafening sound of all those croaking frogs! You couldn't put your foot down without stepping on one. Then as suddenly as they appeared, they began dying everywhere. The dead fish were bad enough. With the frogs, we not only had to put up with the smell, we also had piles of them littering the land."

"But what about those pesky little gnats that came next? There weren't enough swatters in the world to deal with them. And these were signs that God would save us?"

"But the flies were different. And what happened today with our livestock...I wonder...?"

"It's true. Nothing happened here in Goshen but throughout the rest of Egypt there were flies everywhere that completely ruined their land."

"And today the Egyptians' animals were dropping dead where they stood. Horses, donkeys, camels, cattle, sheep, goats—all dead. But in Goshen, every animal lives! I wonder, was Moses right?"

Through three more plagues the question must have laid heavily upon the hearts of the Israelites. When the hail hits and the darkness descends, Yahweh once again makes a distinction between His chosen people and the Egyptians. Not one piece of hail touches the ground in Goshen. And when three days of darkness enshrouds the Egyptians, light shines down upon the Israelites.

But when God tells Moses of the final plague to come, and Moses relays the message, the Israelites are paying full attention. Why? Because the lives of their children are now directly linked with what is to come:

> So Moses said, "This is what the Lord says: 'About midnight I will go throughout Egypt. Every firstborn son in Egypt will die, from the firstborn son of Pharaoh, who sits on the throne, to the firstborn son of the slave girl, who is at her hand mill, and all the firstborn cattle as well. There will be loud wailing throughout Egypt—worse than there has ever been or ever will be again. But among the Israelites not a dog will bark at any man or animal" (Exodus 11:4–7).

> Then Moses summoned all the elders of Israel and said to them, "Go at once and select the animals for your families and slaughter the Passover lamb. Take a bunch of hyssop, dip it into the blood in the basin and put some of the blood on the top and on both sides of the door frame. Not one of you shall go out the door of his house until morning. When the Lord goes through the land to strike down the Egyptians, he will see the blood on the top and sides of the door frame and will pass

over that doorway, and he will not permit the destroyer
to enter your houses and strike you down" (Exodus
12:21–23).

Notice how the people respond this time when deliver-
ance is promised, and the very lives of some of their children
are at stake:

> "Then the people bowed down and worshipped. The Is-
> raelites did just what the Lord commanded Moses and
> Aaron" (Exodus 12:27c–28).

The setting is different, but the method is the same when
we come upon Jairus the synagogue ruler. Most scholars believe that Jairus was probably living in Capernaum, a town
where Jesus had performed numerous miracles. Hence, it is
quite possible that Jairus had heard about, or even witnessed,
some of these supernatural events.

Does this mean that Jairus took the time to sit and learn
at the feet of Jesus? It is doubtful. A synagogue ruler was a
layman who was in a highly regarded position of authority in
the local community. He would be in charge of looking after
the physical building (cf. Luke 4:20) and supervising the order and progress of corporate worship. Choosing who would
read the weekly Torah portions and say the prayers was part
of the immense honor attached to this position.

Synagogue rulers would be in constant contact with the
most highly regarded members of the Jewish communities—
the priests. Undoubtedly Jairus would have had numerous
opportunities to see and hear how many of the scribes and
Pharisees were at odds with the works and words of Jesus.
Taking any time to sit and listen to Jesus, except at the possible request of the scribes and Pharisees, would have meant
occupational suicide. No synagogue ruler intent on keeping
his position of honor would even think of it. Jesus was considered a heretic by the religious establishment.

But what happens when a child's welfare is at stake? Hon-
orable positions mean nothing as a daughter's life hangs in
the balance. Jairus was desperate. He had probably tried every other avenue to have his daughter healed, and none worked.

He fell at the feet of Jesus forgetting all pride and dignity because the need has heightened dramatically.

"My little daughter is dying."

Jairus knows his daughter has reached the final stage and doesn't have much time left. His little girl has just come of age and been declared a woman according to Jewish Law. Twelve years of laughter and love, and visions of her future as a woman, are about to become nothing but a mere memory. Sorrow over the welfare of a child has caused the lives of Jairus and Jesus to merge.

Where previously there may have been an intense curiosity over this miracle Man from Nazareth, He now became the central focus of the synagogue ruler's life.

"Please come and lay your hands on her so that she will be healed and live."

Jairus believed that if Jesus merely touched his daughter, she would live. A considerable measure of faith coming from one who lived in the midst of men who detested the Nazarene prophet. But, his little girl's life was at stake and nothing else mattered. So he came at a dead run to find the Man who he believed could save his only child's life. The welfare of his daughter drove him to seek out the Savior.

But in one short statement from a group of friends, Jairus' hopes appear crushed.

"Your daughter is dead."

Oh what panic mixed with intense grief must have gripped Jairus' soul when he heard those words. "NO, NO, NO! She can't be dead!"

"Why bother the teacher any more?"

Ignoring what they said, Jesus told the synagogue ruler, "Don't be afraid; just believe."

Imagine the thoughts running through Jairus' mind at that moment. "What? Just believe? My daughter is dead. What is there to believe in now?" And yet somehow, somewhere, there is still a spark of hope because Jesus has spoken.

So they press on to see the child.

As they drew nearer to his home, Jairus' chin must have fallen to his chest, shoulders drooped, and his walk turned to a shuffle as he heard the first faint strains of the flutes. "She's really dead!" The flute players only come when death has occurred, hence their name, "the flutes for the dead."

As the mournful wailing of the women filled the air a punctuation mark was placed upon Jairus' nightmare. With each step closer the volume of the mourning grew in intensity. For not only were family members present, but many paid professionals would be on hand to help mourn the loss of this little child. For "even the poorest in Israel should hire not less than two flutes and one wailing woman" (Mishnah). How many more of these professional mourners would be on hand for a prominent family such as Jairus'?

Jesus' response to this raucous display? "Why all this commotion and wailing? The child is not dead but asleep."

The mourners laugh, the parents hope.

By sleep, Jesus was not intimating that the child was merely in some type of comatose state. He was simply letting everyone know that the child's death was only temporary. It's the same word Jesus uses when talking about Lazarus' death (John 11:11–14).

He took her by the hand and said to her, *"Talitha koum!"*

By touching a corpse, Jesus would have become ritually unclean (Leviticus 21:1–4). Apparently that is not an overriding concern for the Healer. He reaches out, takes the girl's hand and says, "Little lamb, I say unto you, arise."

"Immediately the girl stood up and walked around. At this they were completely astonished."

Was that it? Did nothing happen to these parents besides being astonished? What was the rest of the story?

Do you ever wonder what the ultimate effects were of such a fishing trip? Did these parents become servants of the Savior? Perhaps a look at a similar father/child story from the Gospel of John will help answer our question:

Once more he visited Cana in Galilee, where he had

116

turned the water into wine. And there was a certain royal official whose son lay sick at Capernaum. When this man heard that Jesus had arrived in Galilee from Judea, he went to him and begged him to come and heal his son, who was close to death.

"Unless you people see miraculous signs and wonders," Jesus told him, "you will never believe."

The royal official said, "Sir, come down before my child dies."

Jesus replied, "You may go. Your son will live."

The man took Jesus at his word and departed. While he was still on the way, his servants met him with the news that his boy was living. When he inquired as to the time when his son got better, they said to him, "The fever left him yesterday at the seventh hour."

The father realized that this was the exact time at which Jesus had said to him, "Your son will live." So he and all his household believed (John 4:46–53).

Once again a father is prompted to come to Jesus because death is ever-near to a beloved child. The man's official position means nothing compared to the life of his little one. So he begs Jesus to come and heal his son.

"Sir, come before my child dies."

"Jesus replied, 'You may go. Your son will live!'"

When this royal official hears that his son got better at exactly the same time Jesus said, "Your son will live," I'm sure he, like Jairus and his wife, was also astonished, amazed, and overjoyed.

But here, John gives us the rest of the story—the results of the fishing trip.

"So he and all his household believed."

The official and his family came to a genuine faith in Jesus. They had trusted him with their greatest earthly treasure and Jesus provided victory over death. From that day forth, the entire household became disciples of Jesus. Not only was the son healed, but so was his entire family!

Fishing Principle

Show true concern towards the welfare of someone's child and the seed of the Gospel will suddenly have a chance to be planted in the ground of a formerly impenetrable soul. Love a child, cast a net!

STUDY QUESTIONS

1. Take time to reflect and ask yourself if your children are the last thing that often receives your attention. Discuss what the Spirit lays upon your heart. Does a catastrophic event have to occur to turn your heart towards your kids? Take time to praise the Lord when you have made your children a proper priority. Meditate on Psalm 127:3, "Children are a gift from the Lord; they are a reward from him" (NLT), and ask your Heavenly Father to show you new ways to let your children, and other's children, know how special they are in God's eyes - and yours!

2. What would you do if your child's physical life (or any child you're close to) was at stake and God told you how to keep him/her safe? All of our children's eternal lives are at stake. From the moment a child is born, Satan wastes no time trying to woo him/her away from the Kingdom of God. Discuss what you are doing to best ensure your children's chances for eternal life. Take time to meditate upon Deuteronomy 6:4-25, Proverbs 22:6, and Psalm 78:1-7. Pray that you would have the desire and wisdom to take these biblical responsibilities and implement them in your life.

3. Discuss a time when you might have passed up a chance to minister to a child because it was inconvenient or you didn't want to be made "unclean." Take time to repent of your attitude and pray for a softened heart that will make the most of such opportunities in the future.

4. Is there someone in your child's life, a teacher, a coach, youth leader, who has been a godly influence on your child? If yes, take time to call or write that person and thank them for the eternal investment they have made in your child. If no, take time to pray that the Holy Spirit will guide you to such people who can help to plant the seed, water it, and nurture it within your child. Conversely, do you know a child who needs a godly influence in his/her life? Take time to pray that you will be open to the Holy Spirit's leading so you will see opportunities God might use you in to influence that child's life and his/her family.

Scripture

They went across the lake to the region of the Gerasenes. When Jesus got out of the boat, a man with an evil spirit came from the tombs to meet him. This man lived in the tombs, and no one could bind him any more, not even with a chain. For he had often been chained hand and foot, but he tore the chains apart and broke the irons on his feet. No one was strong enough to subdue him. Night and day among the tombs and in the hills he would cry out and cut himself with stones.

When he saw Jesus from a distance, he ran and fell on his knees in front of him. He shouted at the top of his voice, "What do you want with me, Jesus, Son of the Most High God? Swear to God that you won't torture me!" For Jesus was saying to him, "Come out of this man, you evil spirit."

Then Jesus asked him, "What is your name?"

"My name is Legion," he replied, "for we are many." And he begged Jesus again and again not to send them out of the area.

A large herd of pigs was feeding on the nearby hillside. The demons begged Jesus, "Send us among the pigs; allow us to go into them." He gave them permission, and the evil spirits came out and went into the pigs. The herd, about two thousand in number, rushed down the steep bank into the lake and were drowned.

Those tending the pigs ran off and reported this in the town and countryside, and the people went out to see what had happened. When they came to Jesus, they saw the man who had been possessed by the legion of demons, sitting there, dressed and in his right mind; and they were afraid. Those who had seen it told the people what had happened to the demon-possessed man—and told about the pigs as well. Then the people began to plead with Jesus to leave their region.

As Jesus was getting into the boat, the man who had been demon-possessed begged to go with him. Jesus did not let him, but said, "Go home to your family and tell them how much the Lord has done for you, and how he has had mercy on you." So the man went away and began to tell in the Decapolis how much Jesus had done for him. And all the people were amazed (Mark 5:1–20).

Eleven

Fishing
Your Story
with

As I drove up to their house, it was just as I had imagined. Christmas lights in the shape of icicles danced merrily in the night, a wreath on the door gestured invitingly, and the smell of pinion pine blazing in the fireplace wafted through the air. Hurriedly walking to escape the frigid northern night, I suddenly paused.

Perfectly framed by the large picture window was the Johnson family* crowded around the Christmas tree singing carols and properly positioning ornaments. A celebration of the Prince of Peace was underway—I just didn't know it at the time! I was invited by a college classmate to join in these festivities that would forever leave an imprint on my heart.

When the door swung open, I was greeted by five of the most joyful faces I had ever seen. Simultaneously I was hugged, my jacket was hung, and my olfactory senses were bombarded by the feast being fashioned in the kitchen and the cup of wassail placed in my hand. It was a scene straight out of Dickens' *A Christmas Carol,* after Scrooge learns the true mean-

*The names have been changed.

Everywhere my eyes wandered I saw wreaths, bows, candles, lights...It all seemed so perfect. Until I saw the fireplace mantle. There nestled in amongst the garlands was an empty whiskey bottle side-by-side with the family photos.

Soon the entire house was silent. I must have been staring at the bottle longer than I thought. I turned around and the five faces were still smiling.

"Bet you're wondering who puts an empty whiskey bottle on the fireplace mantle between family pictures and an old wooden cross," whispered Mr. Johnson with tears welling up in his eyes. "Let me tell you a story. If you had seen our family a year ago, you wouldn't have recognized us," he continued. "For twenty years, I came home drunk almost every night..."

"I don't need to hear this," I politely interrupted.

"Yes, you do. It's a story that has been told, a story I must continue to tell. I am an alcoholic. But more than that, I was a violent drunk. Rarely a day went by that my wife and kids weren't abused by my screaming and my violent tirades...."

Mr. Johnson paused for a minute to gather his composure while he looked into the eyes of each family member.

"It got so bad that everyday the kids would try to hide in order to avoid my ever-widening abusive path. A tempest was brewing in my soul and I couldn't stop it. I never wanted to hurt my family. I was just out of control. The more alcohol I consumed, the more it consumed me. I was chained to a bottle. Couldn't go anywhere without a drink within arm's reach.

"The reality of the damage I was causing struck a nerve when I came home one night to an empty house. Reaching to open the refrigerator for a cold beer, I found the note."

Dear Mike,

I love you dearly and so do the kids. We cannot, however, continue living in such a dangerous home. We have tried everything we know to help you. Now it's up to you. We need YOU, not what you've become because of the bottle. As long as you drink, you will be living by yourself.

"'Fine, who needs any of you,' I thought. Sitting down to another drink, the house was eerily silent. I felt so alone. Without warning, I began weeping. The weeping turned to sobbing, and the sobbing turned to screaming.

"Sometime afterwards I was awakened by a knock at the door. 'They've come back!' I thought. Much to my dismay, two uniformed police officers stood at the door. Seems the neighbors had reached their limit with my antics, too. People that were once friends had long since abandoned any hope for me. No one even walked on our side of the street anymore.

"In one instant, my anger at the world jettisoned to the surface. One swing at the officers landed me in handcuffs and in county lockup. It was there that the bottle and the cross met head on. Carlos was a police chaplain who spoke with me, prayed with me, and held me over the next three days as I went through withdrawals from the alcohol.

"At the end of those three days, he introduced me to Jesus Christ. He showed me story after story of how Jesus had healed people, people that no one else wanted to be around. People who needed to be 'locked up and the key thrown away.' When everyone else was turning their heads away from this wretched sight, there was One who, Carlos said, was searching for me, diligently seeking me out. I was that one sheep out of a hundred that Jesus so desperately wanted to find and bring home to safety.

"On my knees in a jail cell, Carlos led me in a prayer that changed my life. I cried out to Jesus to be my Shepherd. I cried out to Jesus to be my Savior, and He answered, 'Yes.' I know it's hard to believe, but in that instant I no longer craved alcohol. Life would never be the same. Jesus cured me!

"Carlos called my family and they agreed, with reservations, to come and listen to me. And that's the first time I got to tell the story of what Jesus had done in my life. Over the last year, every member of my family has surrendered their lives to Jesus as they have seen the transformation God has brought to my life. No more crazed, foul smelling, foul talking fool running rampant in the streets. The Prince of Peace resides in my heart and in this home.

brought to my life. No more crazed, foul smelling, foul talk-ing fool running rampant in the streets. The Prince of Peace resides in my heart and in this home.

"The whiskey bottle is empty, but I am finally full."

I wonder if it wasn't similar for the Gerasene demoniac. He hadn't always lived among the tombs. No, he used to live in a house in the local city, but he was no longer wanted. He was an outcast. Demons so overcame his identity that few probably even remembered what their former neighbor used to be like. It was easier to turn the other way, walk on the other side of the street, and forget that this man, too, was created in the image of God.

His dwelling place had been among the tombs for a long time. No one dared go near him anymore because he was "so violent that no one could pass that way" (Mt. 8:28). People feared for their very lives when they were in the vicinity of the demoniac. The constant screaming and wailing that came from the tombs, night and day, was enough, in and of itself, to cause people to give this man a wide berth.

But there was more. All self-control was apparently gone from this man's life. He wore no clothes (Luke 8:27) and his suicidal tendencies were well-documented. Dried sweat and blood are caked on his body from multiple acts of self-mutila-tion: "Night and day among the tombs and in the hills he would cry out and cut himself with stones."

Everyone steered clear of the demoniac's neighborhood in fear for their own safety. The only reason former neighbors had anything to do with this man at intermittent periods was because they wanted to permanently bind him in order to ensure their own safety. "For he had often been chained hand and foot,..." But no matter how many times they tried to control the demoniac, they always failed: "...but he tore the chains apart and broke the irons on his feet. No one was strong enough to subdue him."

Lost among the tombs. Tormented. No freedom in sight. Until one evening when a small boat came ashore. The help-less one was about to meet the Helper.

Can you picture the scene? Jesus' disciples were weary after their storm-tossed venture crossing the lake (Mark 4:35–41). They had just witnessed their Teacher calm the wind and the waves with three words, "Quiet! Be still!" Did this bring them a peace of mind? No. "They were terrified and asked each other, 'Who is this? Even the wind and the waves obey him!'" (Mark 4:41). Hoping for a well-deserved rest, the disciples soon found themselves in the midst of another tempest. Still reeling from the squalls at sea, fear surged through their beings when they heard bloodcurdling shrieks coming from the hills above.

Straining to see in the evening air, they suddenly met with a view beyond belief. A beastlike man streaked onto the shoreline naked. Half-running, half-loping, covered with blood, sweat, and spittle, he dropped at Jesus' feet.

What would you do? I imagine the disciples were fleeing as fast as they could back to the very boat and the very lake they had just been rescued from. They still didn't understand that proximity to the Teacher is the safest place to be!

In contrast, the Healer stood His ground. Jesus reached out to the one that everyone else shunned. Neighbors wanted him banished to lonely places. Jesus wanted to introduce him to lovely places. Jesus still saw the image of His Father in this man. No matter how marred by demons, the image was still there. And Jesus intended to bring it forth to its full glory.

The first step in accomplishing this task was to find out the demon's name. So Jesus asks.

In ancient Eastern thought, it was believed that the first step in gaining control over an enemy was to obtain his name. "From the beginning of time, when God gave Adam the responsibility to name the animals, it is acknowledged that he who knows the name also knows the nature and can therefore control either persons or demons".[1]

---

[1] David L. McKenna, *Mastering the New Testament: Mark,* (Word Publishers, Inc., Lloyd J. Ogilvie, Gen. Ed., 1982) 114,

of demons. But the numbers were great. The man's misery was overwhelming. He was under the control of a host of demons, not just one!

In an instant, Jesus healed the man. "Come out of this man, you evil spirit!" No more demons, no more destruction. Peace reigns! "When they [local people] came to Jesus, they saw the man who had been possessed by the legion of demons, sitting there, dressed and in his right mind; and they were afraid."

Rather than showing excitement over the healing, the neighbors show disdain towards the Healer: "Then the people began to plead with Jesus to leave their region."

Where others kept this man at arm's length, Jesus reached out and embraced him. Is it any wonder that the man who had been demon-possessed begged to go with Jesus? For so long he had been an outcast. Now the One who had freed him was leaving—and at the request of the neighbors. What hope was there at home?

"I want to go with You!"

Jesus' response? "Go home to your family and tell them how much the Lord has done for you, and how he has had mercy on you." Did you catch that? Jesus commanded this man to go and share his story.

Jesus didn't want to leave the people of this region with no hope. Yes, they had rejected him. But he wasn't going away completely. In His great mercy and compassion, He wanted to leave a messenger in His stead. Jesus left them a missionary who had experienced His healing touch.

He would be forever known as the man who had been demon-possessed. It was the perfect bait with which to go fishing. People's curiosity near and far would be heightened at the mere mention of his name. "What was it like? How did you change? Into pigs, huh? Who did this?"

And the man obeyed Jesus' command. He went home and told his story. Jesus didn't command him to preach or teach. He didn't tell the man to try to prove certain theological tenets. NO! He told the man to "tell them how much the Lord has done for you." Tell your story!

His family was the first stop on this missionary journey. Can you imagine their reaction when they heard his voice outside the door? "Quick, hide. He's back!" What fear must have struck at his family's hearts!

But then his wife took a furtive glance outside the window, hoping to not be seen. "He's clean and he's fully clothed. And there's something different about his voice. It really sounds like him."

What an impact it must have had upon the lives of his wife and children! "He lives! My husband and my children's father has returned! Tell us, how did this happen?"

And thus the telling of the story began.

But it did not end there. So filled with thanksgiving and joy was this man that he trumpeted the news to his entire town: "So the man went away and told all over town how much Jesus had done for him" (Luke 8:39).

Lastly, we see him going outside his home town: "So the man went away and began to tell in the Decapolis how much Jesus had done for him. And all were amazed." The Decapolis was a coalition of ten Gentile cities, nine of them located on the east side of the Jordan River, one on the west side. He became a one-man witness throughout this region telling of what Jesus had done. In fact, many scholars believe that Mark saw this man as the first missionary to the Gentiles. His story most likely prepared the way for Jesus' later ministry in the Decapolis (Mark 7:31 ff).

Jesus and His disciples didn't use one method to fish. But one common thread seemed to run through the lives of many that Jesus touched. After meeting the Master, they couldn't help but tell their story. The Gerasene demoniac's effective witness was not an isolated incident.

The Healing of a Man with Leprosy

While Jesus was in one of the towns, a man came along who was covered with leprosy. When he saw Jesus, he fell with his face to the ground and begged him, "Lord, if you are willing, you can make me clean."

> Jesus reached out his hand and touched the man. "I am willing," he said. "Be clean!" And immediately the leprosy left him.

> Then Jesus ordered him, "Don't tell anyone, but go show yourself to the priest and offer the sacrifices that Moses commanded for your cleansing, as a testimony to them."

> Yet the news about him spread all the more, so that crowds of people came to hear him, and to be healed of their sicknesses (Luke 5:12–15).

How did the news of Jesus spread so rapidly that crowds flocked to hear the Good News and be healed of their brokenness? The healed leper was so overjoyed with his encounter that he couldn't help telling others what had happened. "Instead [of not telling anyone] he went out and began to talk freely" (Mark 1:45). This man was so effective at telling his story that Jesus could no longer openly enter a city because of the excitement His presence generated.

It was the most natural thing for the healed leper to do. He didn't have to think about theology. He didn't mull over which method to use. He simply shared his story of being healed by the Great Physician.

Every Christian has a story to tell. Yours may not be as dramatic as the leper or the Gerasene demoniac's, but you do have a story to share. Untold numbers of people can be changed forever by hearing the personal experiences we have had in our encounters with Jesus.

So, what's your story?

> "But in your hearts set apart Christ as Lord. Always be prepared to give an answer [fish with your story] to everyone who asks you to give the reason for the hope that you have" (1 Peter 3:15).

Fishing Principle

*"Go home to your family and tell them {your story}
how much the Lord has done for you, and how he
has had mercy on you."*

STUDY QUESTIONS

1. Why do you think so many pastors start their sermons with a story? Why do you think Jesus told so many parables? Do you like listening to stories? Do you think others do?

2. Remember, not everyone has the dramatic Damascus Road experience of a Paul. Take time to read and discuss the differences between Saul's/Paul's story in Acts 9 and Timothy's story in 2 Timothy 1. Discuss other conversion experiences from Scripture that fall into both of these categories.

3. Take time and share with each other your story of how you met the Savior. When did you commit to becoming a disciple? Where were you when the encounter occurred? What were you doing at that period in your life? Who were you spending time with? Why did you seek out the Savior (or He sought you out) at that point in time?

4. Take time to praise God that you have a story to tell. Pray that the Holy Spirit will help you be sensitive to when He has prepared someone to hear your story. Consider the story of the Gerasene Demoniac and his pattern in telling his story. Pray that you, too, will begin at home and then work your way out into your neighborhood, workplace, city, and beyond...

5. Discuss the phrase, "One person can't make a difference," in light of the effect the Gerasene Demoniac's story had in preparing people to hear the Good News. Pray for the boldness and enthusiasm of the Demoniac (and the Leper in Luke 5:12-15) in sharing your story. Pray for 1 Peter 3:15 to be a reality in your life.

Scripture

Very early in the morning, while it was still dark, Jesus got up, left the house and went off to a solitary place, where he prayed. Simon and his companions went to look for him, and when they found him, they exclaimed: "Everyone is looking for you!"

Jesus replied, "Let us go somewhere else—to the nearby villages—so I can preach there also. That is why I have come." So he traveled throughout Galilee, preaching in their synagogues and driving out demons (Mark 1:35–39).

Twelve

Fishing
with
Prayer

"Should've asked for directions."

Ever wonder why the Israelites had to wander in the desert for forty years? Some say, jokingly, it's because men haven't changed since the beginning of time—they refused to stop and ask for directions.

Unfortunately, many believers, men and women, throughout history, throughout the world, have had the same problem.

How many times have you gone on a fishing trip without stopping to ask God where He wanted you to cast your line? This appears to be the rule rather than the exception for many of us. We attempt to force God to follow us where we have decided to go fishing. Lifting our voices towards heaven, we try to prod God to bless what we have decided to do rather than ask Him to reveal where He is already at work—and then join Him.

The story I shared in the introduction to this book is endemic of this problem. No one prayed and asked God if, or when, we should go fishing on the Riverwalk in San Antonio.

133

"Common sense" merely said that this would be a great place to fish because large masses of men and women would be milling about the banks of the San Antonio River.

Huge crowds. The Gospel. Trained servants. What could be better?

> "No one can come to me unless the Father who sent me draws him, and I will raise him up at the last day. It is written in the Prophets: 'They will all be taught by God.' Everyone who listens to the Father and learns from him comes to me" (John 6:44–45).

Don't get me wrong, there's nothing inherently wrong with fishing on the Riverwalk in San Antonio, Texas. The problem lay in not asking God if that's where we were supposed to be, if that was where He was presently preparing people to hear the Gospel.

Have you ever been on a fishing trip like this? Perhaps you're asked to hit the local shopping mall or local neighborhood on a preset day and time with no prior prayer to see if that's the direction God wants you headed.

There's another way to decide when and where to go fishing. Let's see how Jesus did it.

First, notice when Jesus got up to begin preparing for His fishing trip: "Very early in the morning, while it was still dark...." Three descriptors depict His actions in Mark 1:35: *very, early,* and *in the morning.* Jesus is up before the break of dawn, before anyone else is stirring in the house where He is staying. Based upon the same Greek expression denoting time that is used in Mark 13:35, scholars tell us that Jesus was up somewhere between three and six o'clock in the morning.

"But," you say, "I live an active life. Getting up that early would be a burden, a near impossibility."

I'm not telling you when you should arise to greet the day. I'm simply sharing with you how Jesus prepared for His fishing trip. And, I can guarantee you that the fully human side of Jesus was probably more tired than most of us are on any given morning. Consider all that comprised His previous day:

> They went to Capernaum, and when the Sabbath came, Jesus went into the synagogue and began to teach. The people were amazed at his teaching, because he taught them as one who had authority, not as the teachers of the law. Just then a man in their synagogue who was possessed by an evil spirit cried out, "What do you want with us, Jesus of Nazareth? Have you come to destroy us? I know who you are—the Holy One of God!"
>
> "Be quiet!" said Jesus sternly. "Come out of him!" The evil spirit shook the man violently and came out of him with a shriek.
>
> The people were all so amazed that they asked each other, "What is this? A new teaching—and with authority! He even gives orders to evil spirits and they obey him." News about him spread quickly over the whole region of Galilee (Mark 1:21–28).

On this day before Jesus arises early, we see Him teaching and casting out demons at the synagogue in Capernaum. But wait, the day's not over yet:

> As soon as they left the synagogue, they went with James and John to the home of Simon and Andrew. Simon's mother-in-law was in bed with a fever, and they told Jesus about her. So he went to her took her hand and helped her up. The fever left her and she began to wait on them.
>
> That evening after sunset the people brought to Jesus all the sick and demon-possessed. The whole town gathered at the door and Jesus healed many who had various diseases. He also drove out many demons, but he would not let the demons speak because they knew who he was (Mark 1:29–34).

Think you've had a busy day that precludes arising early? Doubtful any of us have had a day such as this—teaching in the synagogue, casting out demons from an individual at the synagogue, healing a friend's mother-in-law, having an entire town gathered at your doorstep so you can serve them by healing physical infirmities and driving out many demons—until

135

who knows what hour of the night?!! And yet we read that Jesus got up *very, early,* and *in the morning.*

Secondly, notice where Jesus went to prepare for His fishing trip: "Very early in the morning, while it was still dark, Jesus got up, left the house and went off to a solitary place..." Jesus left the house, left the city, and found a place where He could be alone with His Father.

Thirdly, we need to understand why Jesus arose so early and why He chose to go to a site where He would be alone. Remember the crowds that thronged the night before seeking His healing touch? ("The whole town gathered at the door...") One reason Jesus selected a secluded spot was to escape from the crowds and even His disciples. He needed time by Himself, away from other people. He needed time away from those who simply saw Him as the miracle-worker. Jesus needed to be alone with His heavenly Father. Regardless of how busy and exhausting the previous day in Capernaum must have been, He needed time with His Father much more than He needed sleep. He needed guidance to know when and where to fish.

> "For I have come down from heaven not to do my will
> but to do the will of him who sent me" (John 6:38).

Jesus, the man, was dependent on His Father for all things. He only desired to do His Father's will. Hence, He sought His Father's face alone in secret prayer away from the miracle seekers.

How tempting it might have been for Jesus to merely stay in Capernaum. It would have been the easy thing to do. After all, He had just had a successful day performing miraculous healings and exorcisms. And what crowds had gathered! Would this not be a perfect place to go fishing?

Yes—from a common sense perspective.

In fact, Simon and his companions "went to look for" (pursued, tracked down) Jesus in order to tell Him that very thing. "And when they found him, they exclaimed, 'Everyone is looking for you!'" Apparently all the excitement from the previous days' activities had spilled over into the new day. Jesus was still the number one attraction everyone was clamoring for. The disciples themselves may have been awakened by the masses huddled outside of Simon's house waiting for a glimpse of the Prophet from Nazareth. Waiting for a Word, a touch, a chance to be freed from an infirmity.

Simon and his companions wanted Jesus to hurry back to Capernaum to satisfy the cries of the crowds. What an opportunity! Some of these people have also been out searching for Jesus, not content to wait upon Simon's search, and "when they came to where he was, they tried to keep him from leaving them" (Luke 4:42).

Huge crowds. The Gospel. Trained servants. What could be better?

But Jesus knew that the people were not coming to hear about the kingdom but merely to see what the miracle-worker could conjure up to meet their needs. He had received directions from His Father to go elsewhere—"Let us go into the next towns, that I may preach there also."

Imagine the expressions on the faces of Simon and his companions! You can almost hear them say, "What? Now is the time! Now is the place! These people want You. How can you pass up such an opportunity?"

Yes—from a common sense perspective it looked like the time and place to fish. The disciples wanted Jesus to continue performing miracles in order to increase His popularity and His gathering. Jesus' time with His Father, however, had placed an exclamation mark on the fact that His primary mission was not to perform miracles but to redeem the lost: "I must preach the good news of the kingdom of God to the other towns also, because that is why I was sent" (Luke 4:43). *Prayer provides direction.*

In order to experience the power of God in its fullest fruition, we must, like Jesus, be obedient and fish when and where we are told: "So he traveled throughout Galilee, preaching in their synagogues and driving out demons." *Obedience provides power.*

This instance of praying before fishing wasn't merely an isolated incident in Jesus' life. Consider what the Gospel of Luke tells us about Jesus' communion with His Father before the big fishing trip where He chose the twelve to be with Him:

> One of those days Jesus went out to a mountainside to pray, and spent the night praying to God. When morning came, he called his disciples to him and chose twelve of them, whom he also designated apostles: Simon (whom he named Peter), his brother Andrew, James, John, Philip, Bartholomew, Matthew, Thomas, James son of Alphaeus, Simon who was called the Zealot, Judas son of James, and Judas Iscariot, who became a traitor (6:12–16).

Jesus spent an entire night in prayer before choosing the Twelve. ***Prayer provides direction.***

Twelve men were chosen based upon that night of prayer upon the mountain. Men who would be known throughout history—eleven for following the lead of Jesus, one for forsaking his inheritance.

The end result of that prayer? The domino effect was greater than any of them probably ever could have imagined. "These who have turned the world upside down have come here too" (Acts 17:6). ***Obedience provides power.***

If Jesus felt compelled to pray before fishing, how much more important is it for us? Are you too tired to get up early and pray before the day's fishing? Maybe some of us need to consider Jesus' Sabbath day in Capernaum before we say we're too tired.

Sleep has value in the temporal. Prayer has value in the eternal!

Fishing Principle

*Pray before fishing! Follow the promptings of the
Holy Spirit when He calls you to arise and meet
the Master on your knees. Or perhaps your appointment with the Anointed one will be through the
night-watch. Let it not be said of us "You should've
prayed for direction."*

STUDY QUESTIONS

1. Have you ever been through any evangelism training classes/seminars? What was your experience like? Did you have an event to put your training into practice? How did the event go? Was it a success? A failure? How did you determine whether it was one or the other?

2. How often do you, or your local congregation, go on fishing trips without stopping to ask God where He is already at work? Do your actions, the actions of your local church, show that the method or the Master provides success? Discuss why you think that many congregations spend more time focusing on marketing techniques to draw people in rather than time upon our knees? Take time to meditate upon John 6:44-45 and pray that this verse would become a constant companion as you fish.

3. Do you have a regular time when you prayerfully listen for the Lord's leading on the "how, when, where, and who" of fishing? Why or why not? Discuss what the term *prayer evangelism* means to you. Are you using it in your life? How about in the life of your local congregation? Read and meditate upon Acts 16. Discuss the three times that prayer leads to successful fishing trips in this chapter.

4. Does your local congregation have organized prayer times, prayer teams focusing on evangelism? How is your local congregation targeting area neighborhoods? Is there any plan to reach the unchurched, the unsaved? Is there any money in the budget for prayer materials, efforts, etc., in your church's budget?

5. Visualize yourself in Jesus' place as you meditate upon Mark 1:21-39. Take time to pray and ask the Holy Spirit to give you the conviction, desire, and strength to have this type of prayer life devoted to seeking direction for fishing and desire for obedience.

Scripture

Jesus entered Jericho and was passing through. A man was there by the name of Zacchaeus; he was a chief tax collector and was wealthy. He wanted to see who Jesus was, but being a short man he could not, because of the crowd. So he ran ahead and climbed a sycamore-fig tree to see him, since Jesus was coming that way.

When Jesus reached the spot, he looked up and said to him, "Zacchaeus, come down immediately. I must stay at your house today." So he came down at once and welcomed him gladly.

All the people saw this and began to mutter, "He has gone to be the guest of a 'sinner.'"

But Zacchaeus stood up and said to the Lord, "Look, Lord! Here and now I give half of my possessions to the poor and if I have cheated anybody out of anything I will pay back four times the amount!"

Jesus said to him, "Today salvation has come to this house, because this man, too, is a son of Abraham. For the Son of Man came to seek and to save what was lost" (Luke 19:1–10).

Thirteen

Fishing
with your
Treasures

"For where your treasure is, there your heart will be also" (Matthew 6:21).

How many times have you been tooling down the high-way hurriedly pressing on towards your date with destiny—the next appointment scribbled in on your day planner? Suddenly you round a corner and an all-too-familiar sight is up ahead: a broken down car with its stranded driver, arms extended towards the sky, seemingly asking, "Why now?!!"

A prick of your conscience tells you that you should really stop and ask if you can help. Another voice, however, screams louder, "Drive on. Your next appointment awaits!" Without hesitation you ease your car into the lane furthest from the downed vehicle so you don't have to see the face of the fallen one. In an instant, the downed driver becomes a mere blip in the rear view mirror.

A sigh of relief passes your lips as you glance at your watch—"I'm still on time. That was close. I never would've made it if I'd stopped to help."

Sound familiar? It happens everywhere, from big city high-ways to small country by-ways.

Driving in the Texas Panhandle (that would be the small country by-ways for those of you unfamiliar with this region) as the sun begins to set can be one of the most awe-inspiring times of a person's day. A panorama of colors that could be crafted only by the hand of God streaks across the sky. Every cloud seems to literally absorb the reds, yellows, oranges, pinks, and purples until they can't hold anymore.

In stark contrast, the silhouettes of windmills, cattle, and cowboys dot the landscape. Even at 70 miles per hour it's a sight to behold. Until...

Thud! Steam billowed from the engine compartment as our van limped to the side of the road. I never saw it coming. A deer made one leap from behind the mesquite thicket and I smashed into it the instant its hooves hit the highway.

"What was that, Papa?" the concerned voices of our four and six-year olds chimed in harmony.

A glance out the window told them all they needed to know. "Papa, you're not supposed to hit the deer," said our four-year-old with crocodile tears welling up in her eyes.

Our six-year-old had a different agenda, asking, "What are we going to do now? How are we going to meet Mama in Amarillo? Are we going to have to stay here all night? It's getting dark!"

Suddenly I was that stranded driver. Traffic was zipping by me as I looked heavenward with my arms extended. Even on a two-lane highway people attempted to move over to the other lane, eyes fixed forward seeking to keep that next appointment.

They were probably thinking, "I'd stop, but I don't have the time." This phrase often equates to, "It's not a priority."

We all get the same 24 hours per day, the same 1,440 minutes, the same 86,400 seconds. How are we going to use them? Do we have time allotted on our dayplanners for those we say we love? If not, why? Or more importantly, can we put our dayplanners down to make time for those we love?

"For where your treasure is, there your heart will be also" (Matthew 6:21).

Aren't you glad Jesus didn't have a dayplanner? I know Zacchaeus was!

Notice that the passage in Luke 19 says that Jesus was passing through Jericho. He apparently wasn't planning on stopping here, but He saw Zacchaeus on the side of the road and pulled over. He didn't ease into the far lane and pass by: "He looked up and said to him, 'Zacchaeus, come down immediately. I must stay at your house today.' So he came down at once and welcomed him gladly" (Luke 19:5–6).

How astonished Zacchaeus must have been. Not many people wanted to even be near Zacchaeus, much less enter his house. Zacchaeus was one of those detestable tax collectors, a publican. They were viewed by the general Jewish populace as traitors because they worked for the Roman government, and as thieves because they regularly overtaxed their brethren in order to line their own pockets.

Because Jesus wasn't in such a hurry to get to another town, to keep on schedule, Zacchaeus was saved from being stranded along the side of the road. Jesus stopped and helped because He remembered His true destination: "For the Son of Man came to seek and to save what was lost" (Luke 19:10).

The result? "Today salvation has come to this house, because this man, too, is a son of Abraham" (Luke 19:9).

Fishing with time! "For where your treasure is, there your heart will be also." Love is often spelled TIME.

Remember the story of Mary and Martha?

> As Jesus and his disciples were on their way, he came to a village where a woman named Martha opened her home to him. She had a sister called Mary, who sat at the Lord's feet listening to what he said. But Martha was distracted by all the preparations that had to be made. She came to him and asked, "Lord, don't you care that my sister has left me to do the work by myself? Tell her to help me!"
>
> "Martha, Martha," the Lord answered, "you are worried

and upset about many things, but only one thing is needed. Mary has chosen what is better, and it will not be taken away from her" (Luke 10:38–42).

Martha had good intentions but wrong priorities. The preparations took priority over the Person. Are we taking time to be with those we say we love, or are we distracted, worried, or upset about so many things that we "don't have the time"?

Perhaps we all, at times, need to heed some sound advice from the apostles Peter and Paul:

Cast all your anxiety on him because he cares for you (1 Peter 5:7).

Do not be anxious about anything, but in everything, by prayer and petition, with thanksgiving, present your requests to God. And the peace of God, which transcends all understanding, will guard your hearts and your minds in Christ Jesus (Philippians 4:6–7).

What story do our dayplanners disclose? Mary's or Martha's?

As disciples of Christ, we are obligated to not only spend time with the Master but to spend time like the Master— fishing. Is it truly a priority in our lives? When the opportunities arise to reach out do we take them? Or are we too busy?

Remember, Jesus didn't have a daytimer. Time belonged to the work of the Father: "The Lord is not slow in keeping his promise, as some understand slowness. He is patient with you, not wanting anyone to perish, but everyone to come to repentance" (2 Peter 3:9).

Perhaps we all need to take a look at the familiar story of The Good Samaritan to be reminded again of what it means to love with time:

On one occasion an expert in the law stood up to test Jesus. "Teacher," he asked, "what must I do to inherit eternal life?"

"What is written in the Law?" he replied. "How do you read it?"

He answered: "Love the Lord your God with all your heart and with all your soul and with all your strength and with all your mind, and, love your neighbor as yourself."

"You have answered correctly," Jesus replied. "Do this and you will live."

But he wanted to justify himself, so he asked Jesus, "And who is my neighbor?"

In reply Jesus said: "A man was going down from Jerusalem to Jericho, when he fell into the hands of robbers. They stripped him of his clothes, beat him and went away, leaving him half dead. A priest happened to be going down the same road, and when he saw the man, he passed by on the other side. So too, a Levite, when he came to the place and saw him, passed by on the other side.

But a Samaritan, as he traveled, came where the man was; and when he saw him, he took pity on him. He went to him and bandaged his wounds, pouring on oil and wine. Then he put the man on his own donkey, took him to an inn and took care of him. The next day he took out two silver coins and gave them to the innkeeper. "Look after him," he said, "and when I return, I will reimburse you for any extra expense you may have."

"Which of these three do you think was a neighbor to the man who fell into the hands of robbers?"

The expert in the law replied, "The one who had mercy on him."

Jesus told him, "Go and do likewise" (Luke 10:25–37).

Who do you think would have made a better fisherman— the priest, the Levite, or the Samaritan? Which represents our actions when we see people stranded on the side of life's roads?

I can hear some of your arguments now: "Easy for you to say, living on the country by-ways. I live in Los Angeles {or Houston, Chicago, New York}. It's dangerous here."

Life is dangerous everywhere. It was especially so on the road from Jerusalem to Jericho, a seventeen mile stretch through rocky, mountainous territory and desert regions. And it wasn't just the terrain that made it treacherous traveling. Throughout the course of this route there were many caves and hollows where thieves regularly rested waiting for their next victim. Isn't this how we imagine many of our major U.S. cities to be?

So what did the priest do when he saw the victim? He pressed on to his next appointment, failing to see whether he could provide any assistance. After all, if the man was dead and the priest touched him, he would become unclean according to the Law (Leviticus 21:1,11). Here is a man who very likely had just come from performing his sacred duties at the temple in Jerusalem and yet he refused to help his fellow man. He eased over to the other lane and passed by. He used the Law as an excuse to leave rather than an imperative to love— for God commanded the Israelites to show mercy even to strangers:

> "When an alien lives with you in your land, do not mistreat him. The alien living with you must be treated as one of your native-born. Love him as yourself, for you were aliens in Egypt. I am the Lord your God" (Leviticus 19:33–34).

And what did the priest's helper, the Levite, do when he encountered the same man lying in need of help? He followed the example of the priest and eased over to the far lane. Yet before we are too hard on the priest and the Levite, perhaps we should take a look in that proverbial mirror and see where we stand. What do we, "members of the royal priesthood" (1 Peter 2:9), do in similar circumstances? Have we ever passed by someone in need on the way to or from corporate worship services at our local church?

Perhaps we could all learn a valuable lesson from the Samaritan on loving with time. What is the first thing we read the Samaritan did when he saw the wounded man? "He took pity on him." The Samaritan was operating from the heart, not the clock. He had mercy on the fallen one.

For the Samaritan, the destination was not more important than the destitute. Time must be used to help. He pulled over to the side of the road and bandaged the man's wounds, poured on wine as an antiseptic and oil as a salve.

But he didn't stop there! He took even more TIME to place the man on his donkey and take him to an inn where full recuperation is more likely. Once at the inn he spends the entire night caring for this stranger.

Did you notice that the Samaritan didn't show his love merely with his time? He also loved with other treasures—material objects. Wounds were cleansed and treated with the Samaritan's own oil and wine. His donkey was used to carry the wounded one to the inn. And once they arrived at the inn the Samaritan gave the innkeeper two pieces of silver to take care of the man. Not only that, the Samaritan pledged to reimburse the innkeeper for whatever extra was needed to help nurse the man back to full strength!

All this for a stranger. What a fisherman this Samaritan would have made!

Can you truly say that you write no checks to benefit someone, or something, you believe to be important? Or, if you are writing checks, are they becoming proportionately smaller?

Zacchaeus understood this principle when salvation came to his house. Half of his possessions went to the poor. Another wealthy businessman from the twentieth-century, however, had to be reminded that, "Every good and perfect gift is from above, coming down from the Father..." (James 1:17).

Dr. Alan J. Meenan tells the story of the gentleman who was a serious giver to the church. He tithed on all he received and his business was blessed, not as a result of his tithing, but as a result of his faithfulness to God. As his business grew and became more successful, even though he was giving more to God's work, it was proportionately less. He was no longer tithing.

His pastor visited him and said, "Charles, I understand that you are having difficulty tithing."

"Yes," said Charles, who was a good friend of the pastor. "God has blessed my business so much that the amount I would have to tithe is just enormous! I can't afford to pay it any more."

The pastor told him he understood, and asked him to pray with him right there.

"Dear God," he started, and asked Charles to repeat after him. "We love you so much. You have given so much to us." Charles repeated each line carefully.

"You have even given us your only begotten Son. But Father, we have a problem. You have blessed Charles' business so much that he can no longer afford to tithe. We pray that you would make his business less successful so that he will be able to tithe again."

"Oh," said Charles, "I can't pray that!"

The pastor had made his point and Charles began to tithe as an act of obedience to God (sermon, First Presbyterian Church of Hollywood, 1998).

What does your checkbook disclose? Are you a Charles, a Samaritan, a Zacchaeus, or a "poor" widow when it comes to giving to whom or what you love?

> As he looked up, Jesus saw the rich putting their gifts into the temple treasury. He also saw a poor widow put in two very small copper coins. "I tell you the truth," He said, "this poor widow has put in more than all the others. All these people gave their gifts out of their wealth; but she out of her poverty put in all she had to live on" (Luke 21:1–4).

Or are you more like the rich, young ruler when you search your heart:

> Jesus looked at him and loved him. "One thing you lack," he said. "Go, sell everything you have and give to the poor, and you will have treasure in heaven. Then come, follow me."

> At this the man's face fell. He went away sad, because he had great wealth (Mark 10:21–22).

"For where your treasure is, there your heart will be also"

<u>Fishing Principle</u>

Look at your dayplanner and your checkbook. Are time and money being spent fishing? Just as importantly, pull over and help those stranded on the side of life's roads. The dayplanner will still be there when you're done. If you ease into the other lane, the opportunity to fish will disappear in the rear view mirror!

STUDY QUESTIONS

1. Discuss who/what you treasure in life. Would an honest examination of your dayplanner/calendar and your checkbook/credit card statement show this to be true to others? Why or why not? Are we willing to open up our "treasures" to the examination of trusted brothers and sisters in the Lord? Why or why not?

2. Are you more like Mary or Martha? What is a greater consistent priority in your life - the who or the what? Are you more concerned with the "Lord of the work" or the "work of the Lord?" (Dr. Terry Teykl). Read the account of Mary and Martha again. Visual yourself in that room watching Mary, Martha and Jesus interact. Take time and pray that the Holy Spirit would give you a desire to be more like Mary - to choose what is better - to "waste time" sitting at the feet of Jesus.

3. What causes you to sometimes pull over to the other lane and avert your eyes from the ones in need? Have you ever been the one in need who was passed by? Discuss what happened and how it made you feel? Are you more like the priest & Levite, or Jesus & the Good Samaritan, when you see someone stranded on the side of life's roads? Take time to visualize the story of the "Good Samaritan" again. Imagine yourself in each one of the roles as the story is read. Pray that the Holy Spirit would help you to be more like the "Good Samaritan."

4. If you were arrested for being a follower of Jesus, could a court have chance to convict you based solely upon your dayplanner/calendar and your checkbook/credit card statement? Spend this week examining these documents and praying that the Holy Spirit would guide you to use them to help fulfill the Great Commission.

5. Does your checkbook/credit card statement reveal a Charles, a Good Samaritan, a Zacchaeus, a Widow (read Luke 19:1-10), or a Rich Young Ruler (read Luke 10:25-37)? Take time and praise God that He is the One who can change hearts that we might move from being like a greedy Zacchaeus towards becoming like the generous Zacchaeus.

Scripture

Jesus replied, "The hour has come for the Son of Man to be glorified. I tell you the truth, unless a kernel of wheat falls to the ground and dies, it remains only a single seed. But if it dies it produces many seeds. The man who loves his life will lose it, while the man who hates his life in this world will keep it for eternal life. Whoever serves me must follow me; and where I am, my servant also will be. My Father will honor the one who serves me"
(John 12:23–26).

Fourteen

Fishing *with* your Life

"I Love You!"

Words that are so frequently spoken. Words that are so frequently misunderstood.

In order to draw someone near to us, we need to do more than speak those three words. We need to show them what our love means.

Tim Burke understood this principle when he walked away from professional baseball in 1993. Perhaps you've heard his story.

In 1985 Tim Burke's boyhood dream came true the day he was signed to pitch for the Montreal Expos. After four years in the minors, he was finally given a chance to play in the big leagues. And he quickly proved to be worth his salt, setting a record for the most relief appearances by a rookie player.

Along the way, however, Tim and his wife, Christine, adopted four children with very special needs—two daughters from South Korea, a handicapped son from Guatemala, and another son from Vietnam. All of the children were born with very serious illnesses or defects. Neither Tim nor Christine was prepared for the tremendous demands such a family would bring. And with the grueling schedule of major-league baseball, Tim was seldom around to help. So in 1993, only three months after signing a $600,000 contract with the Cincinnati Reds, he decided to retire.[1]

Can you believe that? Our newspapers are glutted with stories of professional athletes who are not content with making six million dollars a year, and here's a man who walks away from a lucrative contract and career. Why?

"Baseball is going to do just fine without me. But I'm the only father my children have," Tim told reporters. Tim understood that saying, "I love you," wasn't enough. He had to show his children what that love meant. He gave up the glamour. He gave up the prestige. He gave up the high life. He gave up the money.

As his children grow, what do you think will mean the most to them about their dad? His 498 professional baseball games pitched? His 444 strike-outs? His 699.1 innings pitched? His 2.72 earned run average? Or the fact that he gave it all up and came home to be with them? Tim Burke hit a grand slam with those four kids when he decided to debut full-time as a dad. Tim gave up his life of baseball, something he had worked for years to attain, in order to sow seeds of love that will forever change the lives of his children.

He went fishing with his life.

A similar scenario took place on a much grander scale, unimaginable by any of us, when Jesus gave up His life in heaven in order to come to earth to help His Father's children. Everyone needs to know they are loved. It's not enough simply to say, "God loves you." People need to have proof.

[1] Dr. James Dobson, *Coming Home,* (Wheaton, Illinois: Tyndale House Publishers, 1998) 16-17.

And God gives it.

> This is how God showed his love among us: He sent his one and only Son into the world that we might live through him. This is love: not that we loved God, but that he loved us and sent his son as an atoning sacrifice for our sins (1 John 4:9–10).

> But God demonstrates his own love for us in this: While we were still sinners, Christ died for us (Romans 5:8).

> For God so loved the world that He gave his one and only Son, that whoever believes in him shall not perish but have eternal life (John 3:16).

> Grace and peace to you from God our Father and the Lord Jesus Christ, who gave himself for our sins to rescue us from the present evil age, according to the will of our God and Father, to whom be glory for ever and ever. Amen. (Galatians 1:3–5).

In order to draw children towards their Father's house, Jesus gave up His life in heaven to come to earth to give up His life on a cross. What are we willing to give up in order to draw people towards the kingdom—in order to fish for our children, our extended family, our neighbors, our workmates?

Jim Elliot, Peter Fleming, Ed McCully, Roger Youderian, and Nate Saint were willing to give up everything, including their lives if necessary, that the Auca Indians might be drawn to God's kingdom. The Aucas lived in the jungles of Ecuador and were feared by all who had approached them over the centuries, and for good reason. As early as 1667, a Jesuit priest who sought to bring the Good News to the Aucas was murdered. In the years just prior to Jim Elliot's and his partners' response to God's call to the Aucas, several employees of Shell Oil were killed while in the Auca territory.

The reputation of this fierce tribe, however, did not deter these five young men. Jim Elliot seemed to sum up their determination to fulfill the great commission when he told his wife, "If that's the way God wants it to be, I'm ready to die for the salvation of the Aucas."

And die they did.

After a few friendly encounters with the Aucas something went terribly wrong. On January 8, 1956, Nate Saint radioed his wife and told her that ten Aucas were coming to their base camp. "Pray for us. This is the day!" Excitement over the ensuing meeting filled Nate's voice.

The next communication with the wives of these five brave men was supposed to occur at 4:30 p.m. that same day. When the appointed time arrived, the radio remained silent.

A Missionary Aviation Fellowship pilot made several passes over the area where the men had made contact with the Aucas. On his fourth flight, he spotted one body that he could not identify. He spotted another body in the river on his fifth pass.

On January 12, Navy fliers went in with helicopters and found four bodies in the river. All had been speared to death by those they were seeking to save.

All around the world people asked, "Why?" The answer came swiftly and the echoes are heard even today by those touched by the story of these five men and their families.

> "I tell you the truth, unless a kernel of wheat falls to
> the ground and dies, it remains only a single seed. But
> if it dies it produces many seeds" (John 12:24).

Many seeds resulted from the deaths of these five young men.

An American naval officer was shipwrecked shortly after reading the story. As he floated alone on a raft he recalled a sentence from Jim Elliot which a reporter had quoted: "When it comes time to die, make sure that all you have to do is die." He prayed for salvation, spiritual and physical. Both prayers were answered.

From Iowa, an eighteen-year-old-boy wrote that he had turned his life "over completely to the Lord." He wanted to take the place of one of the five. Indeed, in succeeding months, missions were deluged with offers to "take the place" of the Auca martyrs.[2]

---

[2]James and Marti Hefley, *By Their Blood,* (Grand Rapids, Michigan: Baker Books, 1978) 619.

The blood shed by these men paved the way for the Aucas to be introduced to Christ. One of their own, a young girl named Dayuma who had escaped from the tribe after they had killed her father, had become a Christian. She went back to her own people to tell them the Good News.

Even the six Aucas who killed the young missionaries eventually accepted Christ as their savior. One of the six became the pastor of the Aucas! Jim Elliot's words were prophetic: "If that's the way God wants it to be, I'm ready to die for the salvation of the Aucas."

But the impact didn't stop here. The sacrificial model of these five men helped spur the Aucas to seek to reach neighboring tribes with the Good News. The Christian Aucas felt compelled to reach a longtime enemy clan down river. Missionaries helped them locate the group. Tona, one of the six killers, volunteered to take the gospel to his down river brothers. Axed from behind, he cried, "I'm not afraid. I'll die and go to heaven."

"We'll help you go," his attackers shouted.

In his dying breath, Tona whispered, "I forgive you. I'm dying for your benefit."

These down river Aucas later came to the Christian community where Rachel (Nate Saint's sister) and Catherine (a Wycliffe Language Analyst) were staying. Many became Christians.[3]

In order to draw someone near to God, we need to do more than speak three words, "God loves you." We need to show them what His love means. Five single seeds fell to the ground. Innumerable plants have been produced.

I recently read of a young man, Stephen Saint, who was stranded in the village of Timbuktu, in Mali, West Africa. Night was falling and he had nowhere to stay. He described the place as the "end of the world." He was a Christian on a fact-finding trip.

[3] Hefley 621

Out of a dark alley appeared a young, handsome man with dark skin and flowing robes named Nouh. He led Stephen to a compound in which he shared with him the fact that years before he had become a believer in Jesus Christ even though it meant that he had become an outcast in his family and their village. His mother had tried to poison him after he had become a Christian.

Stephen asked the question, "Why is your faith so important to you that you are willing to give up everything, even to die? Where does your courage come from?"

Nouh explained that an old missionary had given him some books of other Christians who had suffered for their faith. He said that his favorite was about five young men who willingly risked their lives to take God's good news to the stone-age peoples of the jungles of South America.

"As a matter of fact, one of those men had the same last name as you."

"Yes," replied Stephen, "the pilot was my father." (Dr. Alan J. Meenan sermon, 1998, First Presbyterian Church of Hollywood)

To this day seeds continue to sprout and grow from the fishing trip of those five.

> "The man who loves his life will lose it, while the man who hates his life in this world will keep it for eternal life. Whoever serves me must follow me; and where I am, my servant also will be. My Father will honor the one who serves me." (John 12:25–26).

Both Tim Burke and the five young missionaries, Jim Elliot, Peter Fleming, Ed McCully, Roger Youderian, and Nate Saint, were willing to fish with their lives so that Christ's love would be known. Although Tim Burke did not give up his physical life so that his children would know they were loved by their dad, he did die to his dreams so that the greater good would be served. More of us are daily called to fish with our lives this way than to die a martyr's death.

> "I have been crucified with Christ and I no longer live, but Christ lives in me. The life I live in the body, I live

by faith in the Son of God, who loved me and gave himself for me" (Galatians 2:20).

How many times in a day did Jesus give up creature comforts like rest, sleep, and solitude in order to do His Father's will? Daily, moment-by-moment, Jesus' only thoughts and desires were to fulfill the will of His Heavenly Father. We should be working towards that same goal. That is how we will daily be fishing with our lives.

Or perhaps someday we may be called upon to give the ultimate sacrifice and give up our physical lives to show our Heavenly Father's love to another. "Greater love has no one than this, that he lay down his life for his friends" (John 15:13).

Jesus did just that to show us "God loves you." He knew what it was like to be a missionary in hostile territory. He willingly left His place of honor in heaven to come to the jungles of the earth and bring the Good News in the Flesh to a fierce tribe.

> And they crucified him. Dividing up his clothes, they cast lots to see what each would get.
>
> It was the third hour when they crucified him. The written notice of the charge against him read: THE KING OF THE JEWS. They crucified two robbers with him, one on his right and one on his left. Those who passed by hurled insults at him, shaking their heads, and saying, "So! You who are going to destroy the temple and build it in three days, come down from the cross and save yourself!"
>
> In the same way the chief priests and the teachers of the law mocked him among themselves. "He saved others," they said, "but he can't save himself! Let this Christ, this King of Israel, come down now from the cross, that we may see and believe." Those crucified with him also heaped insults on him (Mark 15:24–32).

Jesus' response?

"Father, forgive them, for they do not know what they are doing" (Luke 23:34).

The ultimate demonstration of the Father's love!

Fishing Principle

Ask yourself who you are willing to die for in order that they might see God's love. Ask the Holy Spirit to show you how you can begin dying to yourself today.

STUDY QUESTIONS

1. Who are you willing to physically die for? Why?

2. Take time to pray. Ask the Holy Spirit to reveal any areas in your life where you might be able to show loved ones their value by dying to something else you consider valuable. Share what ideas the Holy Spirit lays on your heart. Ask the members of your group to pray for you, encourage you, and hold you accountable in seeking to implement these changes.

3. Discuss what you are willing to give up, do without, in order to fish for those who aren't family members – neighbors, co-workers, etc. How can you show others the value you place on their lives and eternal destiny? Take time to pray. Ask the Holy Spirit to guide you in practical ways to "fish with your life" for those outside your family circle.

4. Meditate on Romans 5:8 and Galatians 1:3-5. Take time to praise God for all His grace, mercy and love found throughout these passages.

5. Read and discuss 1 John 3:11-20 and Matthew 5:21-24. Take time to be still and listen to the Lord's leading on how you can improve "loving one another" and fishing with your life. Memorize 1 John 3:16-18.

Epilogue

H arley-Davidson—what pictures do those two words evoke in your mind?

Long-haired men wearing ponytails, earrings, and cut-off jackets with burly biceps as the canvas backdrop for their tattoos?

Probably never thought you'd see Jesus and Harley-Davidson mentioned in the same breath did you? In fact, the word sacriliege might be forming on some of your lips right now.

Occassionally my wife and I get that type of look when we ride up on our Harleys, especially when our girls are riding with us. Some people have a hard time understanding how an ordained pastor and his family could possibly be riding a machine associated with thugs (their words, not mine).

That's okay—a lot of religious people didn't understand or condone Jesus' methods for reaching out to the masses.

Why should it be any different for us today?!!

Realize that all these meditations contain principles that can be used throughout the ages. How they translate to the methods we use will vary from person-to-person and from age-to-age.

Jesus didn't use one method to reach everyone. He was sensitive to individual needs, and we should be, too.

And when I'm at a Harley gathering and see the stereotypical Harley riders intermixed with the yuppies, families, and acne-faced teens, I can't help but think:

"I Wonder if Jesus Would have Ridden a Harley?"